Confident
and
Killing it

TIWALOLA OGUNLESI

Confident
and
Killing it

HQ
An imprint of HarperCollinsPublishers Ltd
1 London Bridge Street
London SE1 9GF

www.harpercollins.co.uk

HarperCollins*Publishers*
Macken House, 39/40 Mayor Street Upper
Dublin 1, D01 C9W8, Ireland

This edition 2022

4
First published in Great Britain by
HQ, an imprint of HarperCollinsPublishers Ltd 2022

HB ISBN: 978-0-00-851801-1
TPB ISBN: 978-0-00-851802-8

MIX
Paper | Supporting
responsible forestry
FSC
www.fsc.org
FSC™ C007454

This book is produced from independently certified FSC™ paper
to ensure responsible forest management.

For more information visit: www.harpercollins.co.uk/green

Printed and Bound in the UK using 100% Renewable Electricity at
CPI Group (UK) Ltd, Croydon, CR0 4YY.

To the women who showed me what it truly means to be unstoppable, my mother Adenike Ogunlesi and grandmothers Elizabeth-White Okuboyejo and Rufina Durogbola Ogunlesi.

And to you, for loving yourself enough to start this journey.

CONTENTS

INTRODUCTION

Have you ever wondered what it would feel like to have unshakeable self-belief? To be able to say, 'This is what I want to do,' and have everything within you – body, mind and soul – conspire to make it happen? That's confidence. It's the belief that you are capable of succeeding in whatever you want to do in life and become whoever you want to be. It's more than a belief, it's a practice, so have hope, because it can be built with awareness and intentionality. Confidence is a never-ending journey. It's a journey that is bumpy at times, but it is the most enlightening, rewarding and life-changing journey you'll ever embark on. Trust me, I've been on it for years now.

Most people think I'm a confidence coach because I've just always been confident my whole life, but it's actually the exact opposite. I'm a confidence coach because I know exactly what it feels like to have a Mean Girl in your mind, a voice that is sabotaging and judgemental of everything you do. I know what it's like to look in the mirror and hate what you see. I know what it's like to live in fear of what others might think. I know what it's like to think, 'You're not skinny enough, talented enough, skilled enough, creative enough.' That was the narrative over and over again. For the longest time I fought to prove to myself and the people around me that I had something to offer. I was an over-achiever and a people-pleaser. I strived to be seen as the 'good girl' because I thought, 'There's nothing special about me, but at least I can make my parents proud by being good.' I thought that was the best I could do.

I was wrong.

My 'wake-up' moment happened when I discovered the world of personal growth thanks to my mum, who gave me a copy of *15 Laws of Growth* by John Maxwell for my 21st birthday.

Now before I go any further, I'd like to say there are actually two parts to my awakening, and I'd be doing my faith a disservice if I didn't talk about the part spirituality played alongside the personal accountability I took in my growth. If you're not a spiritual person or you don't believe in God, that's fine, there's still something to learn from my personal story, so please stay with me and I promise not to shout, 'Repent or die!' through a megaphone.

I was leaving a study room at university when a girl I was holding the door open for invited me to Bible study. Having grown up in a Christian home, I'd been taught to believe that God existed, but I'd never really felt a divine presence. I really wasn't up for 'Kumbaya, my Lord' vibes then, but I was tired and they had my favourite snacks... I entered the Bible study for the free food and left in tears – full-on, snotty-nosed sobbing.

'What happened?' I hear you asking. Well, after some very cringe-making singing, the guy who was leading the Bible study began to read out the following:

'God says you are fearfully and wonderfully made. You are a precious child to Him. When He created you, He said, "You are good." He knows every hair on your head...'

A light bulb went on in my head.

'*Wow*, so you mean when God sees me, all He sees is goodness?'

How was it that the battle I'd been silently fighting all those years was laid out bare in that unplanned moment? I couldn't explain it. But we all have moments when life gives us a wake-up call. Something happens that shakes us up and we begin to realise we want something different – we want more.

That day truly made me start believing that I was created by God, Divine energy and if the Divine being that created me said I was good enough, then *that was final*! No ifs, no buts!

Faith might not be your thing, and I totally respect that choice, but you don't need to have divine intervention to wake up to the truth that you are good enough. That, my friend, is simply a gift you must give yourself.

I let my cup overflow and began to share my greatness with the world. That's the Confident and Killing It effect.

And there's more. Since that day, I've experienced the love, freedom, peace and joy that come from building your confidence. As I started to unlock better versions of myself, the energy that rose within me was too much to keep inside, so I let my cup overflow and began to share my greatness with the world. That's the Confident and Killing It effect.

So what is Confident and Killing It? It's a movement, it's an energy, a mindset, a way of life. It's waking people up to their worth so they can be confident, unstoppable and dare to live the life they truly desire.

How did it start? Back in 2016, I was volunteering as a youth leader and saw just how crushingly low the confidence levels were in the girls I mentored. I realised there was a generational cycle of low self-esteem in women and girls.

In the UK, studies show 61 per cent of 10 to 17-year-old girls have low self-esteem, while 7 in 10 girls believe that they are not good enough or don't measure up in some way, with the most common reasons being their looks, performance in school and relationships with friends and family.[1] If nothing is done about it, insecure teenage girls grow up to become insecure women. Insecure women raise insecure daughters and so a generational cycle of low self-esteem in women and girls is repeated over and over again.

In 2011, the Institute of Leadership and Management in the UK surveyed British managers to see how confident they felt in their professions. Half the female respondents reported experiencing self-doubt related to their job performance and careers, compared with fewer than a third of male respondents.[2]

When it comes to entrepreneurship, the stats aren't too exciting either. Studies show nearly two-thirds of men are confident they can start businesses, but less than half of women feel they have this capability. This is despite similar levels of education and experience.[3]

I found these stats unacceptable so I made it my mission to end this cycle of low self-esteem. I didn't have a huge following on social media, I didn't have any influential connections to lean on, but I did have a voice. So, at the time, all I did was use my voice and share my story. Confident and Killing It started in 2017 as a series of inspiring videos on Instagram, then it grew to become a community of like-minded women, a podcast, corporate workshops, an online learning and coaching academy and now a book! I've spoken in person to women in Lagos, New York, Kigali and Cape Town, as well as all over the UK. I've coached over 120 women who have gone on to get pay rises, start businesses, set better boundaries and level up their life in general. I've run about 100 hours of online workshops with over 10,000 participants. My podcast has been listened to 100,000 times in over 153 different countries in just two years. My confidence tips videos on Instagram have been watched about 1 million times. Now, that's pretty amazing progress for just one woman in five years, but imagine if every single one of you reading this right now joined in and played your part. We could change the world! And why not?

If you've picked up this book it means you're ready to prioritise your growth and wellbeing. It means you're ready to be brave and confront your limitations. It means you're ready to honour your calling and become a better version of yourself. And I'm so very proud of you. So many people find it easier to live in

If you've picked up this book it means you're ready to prioritise your growth and wellbeing. It means you're ready to be brave and confront your limitations.

the smallness of their limitations than in the greatness of their potential, but you're here, you're committed and you're ready to Kill It.

As you'll come to see, it *isn't* about traditional views of success. It isn't about money, fame, power, looking like you have it all together, or overworking yourself for progress 'at any cost'. It isn't about becoming a power woman in a boardroom. 'Killing It' is about defining success on your own terms. It's about knowing you are a co-creator of your life and playing your part to make sure you're living in alignment with your purpose, strengths, passions and values. It's about creating a life that you're proud of – a life at your own pace that works for you. So, read on.

Grounded in the science of positive psychology, this book is packed with practical and proven confidence-building tips, inspiring stories from everyday women and insightful mantras that will empower you to wake up to your true authentic self and overcome limitations like fear, self-doubt, perfectionism and imposter syndrome.

IMPOSTER SYNDROME

Imposter syndrome is a psychological phenomenon where you believe you're an inadequate and incompetent person, despite evidence that indicates you're skilled and successful. You often live in fear of being 'found out' as a fraud or failure, because deep down you don't feel worthy of your accomplishments and opportunities.

You will learn how to believe in your capabilities, bet on yourself, define success on your own terms, embrace your main character energy and prioritise your needs. And as your very own confidence coach, I'm going to be right here with you, guiding you along the way. I'm going to open up your mind to new perspectives, I'm going to help you learn and level up, I'm going to fill you up with energy and drive, I'm going to challenge certain societal norms you've taken as the 'truth' and, sometimes, I'm going to ask you uncomfortable questions.

No more doubting your worth and accepting the bare minimum. No more disqualifying yourself from your dreams. No more mindless hustling to prove yourself. This book is going to awaken something special in you and equip you with next-level confidence that you need to live a full, authentic and empowered life… on your own terms. Are you ready to start?

A lot of us go to personal development to fix ourselves. We think we're broken and so we look to motivational speakers to give us the validation we're so desperately looking for. Well, I'm here to tell you that *you are not broken* and *you don't need fixing*. You are naturally creative, resourceful and whole. This book is not here to fix you, it's here to wake up to the greatness that is already within you.

So, wherever you're starting from is good enough. Your worth doesn't depend on where you come from, how many degrees you have, how much money you have, the colour of your skin, or your sexuality. Your mere existence is a gracious gift to the world. You are one of one. Take a second to feel how special and extraordinary that is.

Here's my number one **#CAKIMantra**:

You matter simply because you exist.

You'll come across more of these nuggets of wisdom as you read through this book. Feel free to write them out, put them on sticky notes, tweet them or make them your screensaver. They're here to remind you of what it means to be Confident and Killing It.

Real societal change starts on an individual level, and real societal change is needed. Even with more women getting degrees these days we still get paid less and miss out on promotions. We've been sold a lie that if we just work harder, don't make a fuss and let our work speak for itself we will be noticed and rewarded. If you're waiting for your manager to give you a pay rise instead of asking for one, because you think once they see how hard you work, they'll know you deserve more, then, girl, bye, you'll be waiting forever. People can see when you deserve more, but they'll often offer you less just to see how confident you are in yourself. However you respond is the baseline they'll use for how to treat you moving forward. I hope that makes you think twice the next time you think about playing small.

Looking at these stats (pages 15-16) can be quite disheartening. There are so many societal barriers to women's confidence that you might be thinking, is there any hope?

CONFIDENT AND KILLING IT

YOU MATTER SIMPLY BECAUSE YOU EXIST

#CAKIMantra

There is.

We can start with working on the things we have control over. Things like internalising rejection, pursuing perfectionism and fearing failure are self-inflicted confidence killers. We can make a choice not to give them power. The focus of this book is self-mastery, which involves knowing and growing yourself. We won't just focus on 'improving' you by forming new habits that rewire your brain for success; we'll also being doing loads of self-exploration and self-acceptance. Instead of sabotaging ourselves, we can own our truths, our voices and our stories, because when we do, change happens, ceilings are smashed and lives are changed.

On the other hand, I'm also not putting all the responsibility on us women to break the cycle when we've seen that many women experience societal backlash for being unapologetic about their worth. I admit there are some things beyond our control, but are we going to sit around and wait for the world to just magically be a better place before we build confidence? No. As an adult, your confidence, like many other things, is your responsibility.

I also want to highlight that issues like imposter syndrome and low self-esteem aren't only women's issues. Men doubt themselves too. They aren't superhuman. Katty Kay and Claire Shipman have studied the confidence gap between women and men in their book *The Confidence Code*. In it they explained that most men don't let their doubts stop them from taking action. Doubt is often a catalyst for action. And when they experience failure after taking action, they most likely blame their lack of effort – 'I didn't work hard enough' – or attribute it to external circumstances – 'That was a tough exam' – whereas women put the blame on a lack of skill and capability – 'I'm not smart enough.' Women also tend to feel the fear and retreat, overthink situations and then never take action. Sound familiar?

But the more we hesitate, trying to avoid failure by waiting for the perfect moment to act, the fewer opportunities we have to build our confidence, and when we don't build our confidence, we are more likely to hesitate. It's a vicious cycle. I'm sure you've heard of the popular stat from Hewlett-Packard that showed women applied for a promotion only when they met 100 per cent of the qualifications, while men applied when they met 50 per cent. Feeling we're not good enough leads to less risk-taking in order to avoid any sort of failure, shame or judgement, and as a result we take fewer opportunities outside our comfort zone, opportunities that could have built our confidence.

Just because there's a confidence gap between women and men doesn't mean we fix it by thinking or acting like men. The good news is no matter who you are or what personality you have, confidence is something you can nurture and express in your own style. I will give you the framework and tools to build a solid foundation. The rest is up to you. Throughout the book you'll come across what I call 'Level-Up exercises'. These are exercises to help you grow in your self-knowledge. To get the best out of this book, I recommend completing each exercise before moving onto the next chapter and using a designated journal or digital notepad to write your answers down so you have them all in one place.

For the longest time, traditional psychology has studied human pain and suffering in the hope that if we know how to manage these situations, we can alleviate them and be happy. However, positive psychology takes things one step further and looks at the science and intentionality behind boosting our wellbeing so we can live a full and rich life. The PERMA model, created by the father of positive psychology, Dr Martin Seligman, presents five pillars of wellbeing that have been scientifically proven to help us manage our emotions, feel passionate about our work, develop meaningful relationships, live out our purpose and celebrate our accomplishments.

PERMA

PERMA stands for

P – Positive Emotions

E – Engagement

R – Relationships

M – Meaning

A – Accomplishments

I'll be introducing the five pillars to you in more detail throughout the book, alongside simple and practical ways to apply them in your life. Happiness is a moment in time. Wellbeing is about having the tools to thrive and flourish no matter what life throws at you, and that's the foundation this book is built on.

I wholeheartedly believe every single woman and girl out there deserves to love and believe in herself. It's not a 'nice-to-have' or something for a select few in society. No. Loving yourself and believing in your worth is a birth right and I won't stop fighting for it until confidence in women is the norm rather than the exception. Are you ready to join me on this journey?

DISCOVERING YOUR AUTHENTIC SELF

Growth starts from sitting with yourself in the present moment and exploring what's there. You cannot improve on or heal from what you do not acknowledge, so the first step to building confidence is to become aware of our current situation, your strengths *and* your limitations.

In this chapter I'm going to guide you from a fixed mindset to a growth mindset. This journey will help you wake up to your true authentic self. Authenticity is about being brave enough to be yourself and genuine enough to live according to your values. What you say and what you do must be in sync with what you truly believe.

Here are some fixed mindset traits. If you feel you resonate with any of these, then welcome to the party, you're in the right place and you are not alone.

Authenticity is about being brave enough to be yourself and genuine enough to live according to your values.

A FIXED MINDSET

Leads to a desire to look smart and a tendency to:

- Avoid challenges and always want life to go very smoothly.

- Give up easily in the face of obstacles.

- See effort as pointless and prefer immediate gratification.

- See no value in expressing emotions freely and clearly.

- Want to be loved by everyone and not be open to learning from mistakes.

- Feel threatened by or jealous of the success of others.

- Have a scarcity mindset and believe there's only room for one person to win.

This was me. I ticked every single one of these boxes. On the surface it looked as though I was winning. I was the good girl who did well in school, I always followed the rules so that people would love me and I did everything in my power to look as though I had it all together, but behind closed doors, if things didn't go as planned, I would fall apart. Essentially, I was far from being my authentic self.

If this is you right now, please don't freak out or get stressed. This is actually a very exciting moment for you, because it's an opportunity to see the signs of what an authentic life is and isn't. A fixed mindset breeds inauthenticity because in order to please everyone, ignore constructive criticism, avoid challenges and obsess over looking perfect, you have to play safe, play small, be judgemental and hide parts of yourself to live up to other people's expectations. This is what it feels like to live an inauthentic life. It might not seem like a big deal if you do this from time to time, but continuously living a lie in order to be accepted, or alternatively, being judgemental towards others while thinking you're perfect will have long-term effects on your mental health, emotional health and overall fulfilment. It will leave you feeling empty with regret. And that is not #goals.

HOW YOU'VE BEEN SHAPED BY THE WORLD AROUND YOU

We are constantly bombarded with messages that tell us happiness is found in material things. If you buy this cream, you'll feel worthy, or if you buy this car, people will respect you. We live in a patriarchal capitalist society that thrives off our insecurities. Most of our 'flaws' that apparently need fixing were conjured up by old white men in a marketing suite brainstorming ideas on how to keep women buying products in the name of self-love. Capitalism has created a 'perfect' image of a woman that is so unattainable that some women end up spending all their lives (and money) in the pursuit of something they will ultimately never achieve.

With all this in mind, it's no surprise that so many of us have grown up thinking we're not good enough and feeling the need to fight every day to prove our worthiness. But though our insecurities may not be our fault, it is our responsibility to figure out a way to love ourselves and create our own truth despite all the marketing messages around us. There comes a point in our life where we can no longer blame our parents, teachers, friends or society for our shortcomings and we have to take ownership of our life, our dreams and our choices.

If you're not happy with the life you have right now, the good news is you can create a version that works for you, a version based on *your* truth and vision, which is exactly what we're going to do in this chapter.

From the moment we're born, we're swimming in a massive sea of human beliefs, truths, ideas and practices. Some are expansive and make us feel free; others are unnecessary, limiting and sometimes even crippling. Unfortunately, it's often the dysfunctional and crippling truths that tend to be the loudest in society and stick in our heads.

In the book *The Code of the Extraordinary Mind*, author Vishen Lakhiani explains how a lot of the 'truths' that society tells us to believe about ourselves are relative truths and are waaaay past their expiration date. By 'relative truths', he means ideas, concepts, laws and beliefs that are only true for a particular culture or tribe. For example, the rules around what's acceptable when it comes to marriage are different across cultures. They aren't true for every single human being on the planet. They *are* true for the people who *choose* to believe in them. 'Truths' like 'Your worth is based on your productivity', 'You have to be married with kids by 30' or 'You shouldn't wear a bikini if your tummy isn't flat' are also relative. They might be true for *some* people, but they certainly don't have to be true for *you*.

One of the keys to being Confident and Killing It is knowing what truths serve you and what truths don't. For example, believing you aren't good enough for the opportunities you want doesn't serve you.

When I started my personal growth journey and learned that growth was intentional and I had the power to define myself and my future on my own terms, it became clear to me that the narrative that I wasn't talented, skilled or creative wasn't loving or right and didn't feel good. So, I decided to let it go and *create* a new truth. I put my limiting beliefs to the test and found out that everything I believed about who I was and what I was capable of was a lie. Today, I believe that I am creative, gifted, one of a kind, a generational leader, resilient... The list goes on.

Our primary duty is to create our own truth and go about the business of living it. So, now it's time for you to create your new truth.

HOW TO CREATE YOUR OWN AUTHENTIC TRUTH

Here are five practical steps you can take to create your own authentic truth and build a strong foundation of confidence:

 Step 1:
Identify and articulate your strengths

 Step 2:
Deep dive into your passions

 Step 3:
Define your values

 Step 4:
Unlock your Power Circle

 Step 5:
Create your purpose

These steps are an integral part of the journey you're embarking on in this book and are fundamental to increasing your self-awareness and confidence. Confidence is a skill everyone can learn, so let's get started!

STEP 1:

IDENTIFY AND ARTICULATE YOUR STRENGTHS

CONFIDENCE CHECK-IN: A LOOK INTO YOUR MIND

Time yourself for one minute and write down as many of your strengths as you can think of, then for another minute write as many weaknesses as you can think of.

- O   Which came easier to you?

- O   Which do you have more of?

Knowing your strengths is arguably the most important aspect of building confidence and is often the most overlooked step. Your strengths act as the foundation for the thoughts you have about yourself. They also make you feel more secure in your worth.

So, take a moment and think about what's going on in your head. If you know your weaknesses better than your strengths, it means you're operating from a place where you don't feel good enough, a place that feels really negative and critical, instead of a place where you know you're good enough. You're not alone.

When I ask people to tell me what their strengths are, they're always looking left, right and down, hoping now is a good time for the ground to open up and swallow them. The first response is hesitation, every single time. But when I ask them to tell me what their weaknesses are, oh boy, the way they roll off their tongue: 'I'm so bad at this, I'm so awkward at that, I'm always late...' The list goes on and on.

CONFIDENT AND KILLING IT IN ACTION

One of my clients, Anna, a qualified medical doctor who runs a successful cosmetic and skincare clinic, suffered from this. She got nothing but glowing feedback from her clients, her referrals were through the roof, she barely did any advertising and could still own her own space in an esteemed neighbourhood in London. Yet after each session all she could see were all the things she could have done better for her clients. She was hyper-aware of her limitations and completely oblivious to her strengths.

Does that sound familiar?

The first thing I did with Anna was ask her a series of questions to help her see all the greatness inside her. She started the session only aware of about three strengths and left with 30! Life-changing. You will soon be completing these questions for yourself.

Knowing your strengths doesn't just boost your confidence, it also helps you overcome fear and insecurities like imposter syndrome. Are you surprised you tend to feel like a fraud when you have no idea of what you're good at doing? You walk into rooms, a shell of yourself, wondering how you got in there. Sis, stop sleeping on yourself. Again. Stop. Sleeping. On. Yourself.

When you know your strengths, you're aware of what you bring to the table, and you won't let anyone take you for a fool. The world or your negative thoughts might try to convince you that you're nothing special, but because you're awake to your greatness, you don't let it stick. You're bold enough to challenge it with the truth of who you really are.

If you struggle to own your strengths, please don't beat yourself up about it. This is another wake-up moment for you to decide how you want to show up from this point on.

Let me unpack a little why you might struggle to own your strengths and help you to reframe it. The first reason may be because you think strengths are things you are *perfect* at doing. If you think you're organised, for example, you may think you need to be organised every single moment of your life for it to be considered a strength. That's not true. You are human, and

Knowing your strengths doesn't just boost your confidence, it also helps you overcome fear and insecurities like imposter syndrome.

perfection doesn't exist. There will be days when you are fiercely organised at work but your life admin is a bit of a mess, that doesn't take away from the fact that organisation is one of your strengths. Or maybe you're a pretty reliable person and you often keep your word, but on a few occasions life hasn't gone as planned and you've had to let people down. Guess what? Being reliable is still one of your strengths.

Don't be so quick to cancel yourself, give yourself some grace and see your strengths as a sort of treasure chest inside you. You can activate this amazing bank of resources at different moments in your life. They might not always be switched on, but they are always there.

The second reason people struggle with strengths is they tend to think, 'If there are people out there who are better than me at it then it can't be my strength.' For example, 'I'm not creative' is something I hear a lot from my clients and also something I used to believe about myself. People often say they aren't creative when they look at themselves in comparison to others or if their creativity doesn't come in a mainstream form like writing, dancing, drawing, painting, singing or playing an instrument. However, creativity is really broad and shouldn't only be limited to those mainstream expressions. We're all inherently creative – think daydreaming, problem-solving, or dressing – it's just that some people start exploring sooner and give themselves opportunities for their creativity to manifest into something. For example, my brother, Gboyega, started expressing his creativity through music and technology at the age of seven. He could take computers apart and reassemble them by the age of 10 – a genius really! My sister, Mowa, started expressing her creativity through

Your strengths are your strengths in relation to you, your life and your journey.

fashion and art at the age of 11. She could draw, paint, make handbags, you name it. I finally came to terms with my creativity through my spoken and written words at the age of 25, but before then even though I was an incredible problem-solver and dancer, I struggled to think I was creative because I couldn't draw, paint or play an instrument like my siblings. That was a form of sabotage. In reality all three of us have creativity as a strength, even though that strength is applied in three different ways.

So, your strengths aren't your strengths in relation to someone else. Your strengths are your strengths in relation to you, your life and your journey. There's enough room for all of us to have the same strengths; it's not a competition.

The third reason why I see people struggling to embrace their strengths is that they think it's boastful or arrogant. This is the one that really breaks my heart, because it is pure brainwashing. Our patriarchal society wants women to run from their greatness so that they never unlock their full potential and step into their power. They prefer to have us asleep on autopilot, passive and submissive, because when we are, they can call the shots and exclude us from important conversations. So, hun, we really need to stop this insecurity Olympics. There is no award for being the most insecure person.

Have you noticed when a group of women are together it's almost like there's a competition for who has it worse?

Woman 1:   *'I've noticed you're really good at thinking on your feet.'*

Woman 2:   *'OMG, it's honestly luck. I'm so jealous of how good you are with people. I'm terrible at that. I'm so awkward.'*

Stop it! Owning your strengths is not arrogance. *It's not bragging if it's a fact.* It's a fact that I'm resilient. I have evidence and proof of it. I know it's not something to hide, it's something to embrace. It's a fact and it's more likely to inspire other women than make them insecure, because if I can do it, they can do it too.

Your strengths truly are the foundation for your confidence, and the Level-up exercise on pages 38-42 will help you to identify and articulate them. Once you've done that, it's time to get intentional about living them out. Because when you use your strengths every day, you're more likely to make progress, grow and feel good about yourself. When you feel good about yourself, you're more likely to take action, because you feel you're going to succeed. You'll feel more confident owning your truth when you know it's grounded in the reality of your strengths, gifts and skills.

LEVEL-UP:

ARTICULATE YOUR STRENGTHS

Here's a table of strengths to help spark some ideas, in case you get stuck answering the questions on the following page.

Active	Caring	Determined
Adaptable	Cheerful	Disciplined
Adventurous	Compassionate	Dynamic
Ambitious	Confident	Efficient
Articulate	Considerate	Eloquent
Athletic	Cooperative	Empathetic
Balanced	Courageous	Encouraging
Brave	Creative	Energetic
Calm	Cultured	Enthusiastic
Capable	Curious	Ethical
Captivating	Daring	Faithful

Far-Sighted	Lovable	Resilient
Flexible	Loyal	Resourceful
Focused	Mature	Respectful
Forgiving	Meticulous	Responsible
Free-Thinking	Nurturing	Self-Aware
Friendly	Objective	Selfless
Fun-Loving	Observant	Sensitive
Generous	Open	Sociable
Genuine	Open-Minded	Skilful
Hardworking	Optimistic	Sophisticated
Helpful	Organized	Spontaneous
Honest	Passionate	Strong
Humble	Patient	Supportive
Humorous	Persuasive	Sympathetic
Imaginative	Positive	Talented
Independent	Practical	Thoughtful
Innovative	Productive	Trusting
Insightful	Punctual	Understanding
Intelligent	Purposeful	Vivacious
Intuitive	Rational	Well-Rounded
Kind	Realistic	Wise
Leaderly	Reflective	Witty
Logical	Reliable	

1. **What do you naturally excel at?**

   What comes naturally to you? What can you do with ease, without having to try too hard? For example, I'm a natural problem-solver. People always come to me for advice. Maybe you're always organised – you're on time, you have plans or processes laid out in a logical order and you have back-up plans if things go wrong.

2. **What work energises you?**

   What skills do you use that make you feel good after you've used them? What can you often do for hours without realising? For example, if you always get lost in brainstorming creative ideas, you're a creative thinker. Personally, I'm always buzzing after events and workshops, and when I'm speaking to groups of people, I feel energy rising within me. This tells me verbal communication is one of my strengths.

3. **What do people compliment you and praise you for?**

   Think of the positive feedback you've had from colleagues, managers, family and friends. If you're struggling to write something down, get on the phone and ask someone you *trust and respect* what they think you're good at doing. The emphasis here is on making sure that this is from someone you trust and respect. Not everyone can see your strengths, so make sure you ask the right person.

   For example, maybe you're always the calm and positive voice of reason when everyone is freaking out. So keeping your head is one of your strengths. Or you're very thorough in your work from start to finish. In that case, attention to detail is one of your strengths.

4. What do you do to add value to people and help them?

Life isn't just about you, you, you. You can learn a lot about your skills and gifts from how you support other people. I discovered my gift for speaking and drive for social impact when I was volunteering as a youth leader with my local church. If you're really good at being there for your friends, then being supportive and reliable could be some of your strengths. Maybe you're really good at helping people get through challenges. If so, being a problem-solver could be one of your strengths.

5. Think of a moment when you were proud of yourself, big or small. What strengths or skills were you demonstrating in that moment?

For example, graduating from university, or getting your first job or perhaps overcoming a challenge. What strengths did you demonstrate to get to that point? If you've survived all the challenges that have come your way, I'm pretty sure you can put down resilience as one of your strengths.

Keep a note of all the strengths you've come up with and create a strengths log either in your confidence journal or your digital notepad. I use Google docs, for example. Whenever you discover a new strength, go write it down in your log.

Now if you really want to level up, go the extra mile with these two bonus steps:

1. For every strength write down *why* you believe you have that strength

2. Add *an example* of when you've demonstrated that strength, by using the following formula:

   I am… because…

   A time I showed this strength was when…

   For example: *'I am resilient because I can bounce back from challenging situations. A time I showed this strength was when the pandemic hit and I lost all my clients and bookings, managed to rebuild and saw more growth than I'd ever seen before.' (More on that later.)*

Knowing your strengths is just the first step, knowing why that strength is yours and a tangible example of when you've displayed that strength will take your confidence to the next level! If you have multiple examples, write them all down – more is best in these situations.

Now you may be thinking, 'Tiwa, why do I have to do this?' Well, the answer is because when that loud and critical Mean Girl in your mind goes, 'Are you *really* resilient? Remember that time you got rejected and cried like a baby – that doesn't look like resilience to me,' what will you say? You've got to come with the receipts!

STEP 2:

DEEP DIVE INTO YOUR PASSIONS

It's now time to articulate your passions. Your passions are the things that energise you and set your heart on fire. They're your life's fuel.

I truly believe life is abundant and vast, and passion is the same. Passion isn't static, it's dynamic, so at different seasons or stages in your life, you will have different passions. Don't be so focused on finding *one* passion that you miss all the other joys in your life.

Grace Beverley said it best in her book *Working Hard, Hardly Working:*

> 'We need to widen the scope of what passion means and live in a way where we insert smaller passions into the everyday, rather than try to fit the complexity of our everyday needs into a single passion.'

How is following your passions linked to confidence? Well, when you spend your time doing what you're passionate about, you have a glow about you, you're energised and loving life. This energy gives you the motivation you need to try new things, go after your goals and take risks. When, on the other hand, you choose money over passion or pleasing people over fulfilling your own needs, you often end up in a situation where you are surviving instead of thriving. Everything is such an effort. So you feel demotivated and are less likely to pursue your goals.

So, the next time you want to commit to something, whether it's a job, business project, or even a relationship, ask yourself: 'Is this really in alignment with what sets my heart on fire?'

When I graduated from university, I thought being a passionate person meant I could make any job work for me. So I took the first offer and ended up moving to Oxford to work for an engineering company that sold plastic components – plugs, Printed Circuit Boards and other bits and bobs that went into cars, fridges and printers. Yeah. Imagine the Tiwalola you know now working in the marketing department of this kind of company. My so-called 'passion' lasted all of three days. Having to sell products I cared nothing about was absolute torture, and it drained me. I would come home from work crying my eyes out every day because my soul felt empty. Forgoing passion for money or the approval of others is never worth it in the long run.

Now I know some of you are already shouting at me, 'What if my passions don't pay the bills?' or 'What if my day job doesn't have room for my passions?' That doesn't mean you should forget about them. Not every passion needs to be monetised, and you can't wait for people to give you permission to express yourself creatively. Creative expression is essential to your wellbeing, so think about how you use your free time. Don't spend your whole evening watching TV and get mad at yourself for having no time to follow your passions. You have to *make* the time.

LEVEL-UP:

IDENTIFY YOUR PASSIONS

The following three questions will help you to identify your passions:

1.   What do you talk about?

What lights you up whenever you hear someone talking about it? What could you yourself go on and on about for ages? If I woke you up in the middle of the night and said, 'Tell me about xyz,' what would you happily talk to me about?

For me, it's personal growth, travel, health, relationships, economic empowerment for women (no surprise there), self-care and definitely Beyoncé.

_____

_____

_____

_____

_____

_____

_____

_____

2. What do you cry about?

What makes you so angry you want to do something about it? What's a problem you're really passionate about solving?

I admit the idea of there being a generational cycle of low self-esteem in women and girls really, really upset me! We deserve to love ourselves and it breaks my heart when I hear the stats: 85 per cent of women and 79 per cent of girls state that they've chosen not to do important life activities – such as trying out for a team or spending time with loved ones – when they don't feel good about the way they look.[1]

_____

_____

_____

_____

_____

_____

_____

_____

_____

_____

_____

_____

_____

_____

_____

_____

_____

_____

_____

3. What do you daydream about?

What do you lose time thinking about? What do you visualise when you think of your life and your future?

I daydream about building a global media company that focuses on helping women build confidence. I cannot tell you the number of times I've seen myself doing book tours all over the world and walking into stadiums filled with women screaming, 'Confident and Killing It.' I dream about creating my own TV show where I mix personal development with travel (my two favourite things). I dream of having a Japanese-inspired garden in my dream house so I can achieve new levels of zen. And I dream about leaving a legacy and the impact my work will have long after I'm gone.

Your answers will all point towards your passions. These are the things that make you feel alive, and when you live them out, it builds your confidence. Passions don't always have to be monetised and turned into a business – you can have a wide variety of passions and hobbies and that's OK! Some passions can be found in your work life and some passions can be found in play.

Another popular question in my coaching sessions is: 'I'm passionate about so many things – how do I know which one to pursue?' My answer to that is to look for common themes across the passions. Passions aren't only topics like politics, travel, food and theatre. They can be more contextual, like problem-solving or social change. For example, if you look at my Instagram you'll see that I'm passionate about empowering women, travelling and self-care. Now I don't have three businesses, one for each passion. Only one of those is a business, but the thing that brings all my passions together is that in each one of them I express my love for living life to the fullest. Call me an expert at enjoying life [clink clink], but that's a passion too.

CONFIDENT AND KILLING IT IN ACTION

In one coaching session, a client, Emma-Louise, expressed her love for politics, sex education, writing and presenting, and was stuck on which one to make her main career. Should she be a presenter on the BBC? Should she be a podcast host? Should she be a political writer? Ohhh, so many options. Can you relate?

After we went through steps 1 and 2 in the previous exercise to help her identify her strengths and passions, we concluded her underlying passion that brought all these things together was her love for bringing taboo topics into mainstream media and having powerful conversations about them. So whether it's conversations about women in politics or sexual liberation, her job is to find a way to have meaningful conversations, which can be done through a host of mediums.

Another example of how multiple passions can be pulled into a single thread comes from a woman called Femi, who approached me in my co-working space to tell me how much she loved my lockdown webinars..

We got talking and naturally I asked her about what she was into, and as she told me about her love for music and technology, I began to notice a theme. Although she had multiple passions, the context bringing them together was her love for taking complex ideas and breaking them down into everyday language. In tech she was passionate about breaking down barriers to entry and turning tech lingo into plain English so the industry could become a more diverse space. In music she loved analysing the lyrics, melodies, and meaning of a song in depth and then breaking it down in conversation with other music lovers. Simplifying ideas was her real passion and it played out in many different areas, she didn't just have to choose just one.

What started out as a bit of small talk about passion and drive presented itself as a great real-life example that if you've got multiple passions, you're not alone.

Bestselling author and podcast host Emma Gannon also supports the idea of having multiple passions in her book *The Multi-Hyphen Method*. She says, 'being a multi-hyphenate is about choosing and strategising a plan of attack and having the freedom to take on multiple projects, not being backed into a corner. This is about choosing a lifestyle. This is about taking some power back into our own hands.'

So if you want to, you can design a career that pulls your various passions into a cohesive whole that gives you flexibility and career longevity. A 'multi-hyphenate' lifestyle allows you to explore and express all areas of your personality. So there you have it, you don't have to pick one passion and focus on it for the rest of your life. You can if that works for you, but for many of us there are so many parts of ourselves we want to explore. Don't hold back – there are no limits or rules. Do what feels good, right and loving for you, and if you feel you're spreading yourself too thin, reel it in a bit. This is the art of authentic living.

STEP 3:

DEFINE YOUR VALUES

The third part of creating your authentic truth is about understanding why values are important, learning how to define them and finding fulfilment by honouring them. In this section we're going to look at what values are and how to identify your own core values.

Values are defined as 'principles or standards of behaviour, one's judgement of what's important in life'. When you feel there's something missing in your life, or you're lacking motivation, you're unfulfilled or stuck, it's often because there's a value or set of values you're not honouring. Part of living as your true authentic self is to know what's important to you, what you want to stand for, the kind of person you want to be, and to honour all of that.

Knowing is easy, but actually creating time to *do* what's really important is something we all struggle with. Wellness is important to me, for example, but I struggle to meditate. Faith is important to me, but I struggle to carve out quiet prayer time. But going for brunch? I'm there. (Awkward admitting this in my own book, but there we have it – I'm keeping it real.)

CONFIDENCE CHECK-IN: DOING WHAT MATTERS

○ Take a moment now and take stock of your life.

○ Make a list of all the things that are important to you and track how much time you spend doing those things.

It's very likely that you spend more time doing things you're not that bothered about, for example scrolling on social media, and less time doing the things you really enjoy, for example going for a long walk, reading a book or doing your nails. Our capitalist patriarchal society has a way of sucking us into mundane autopilot living, and if we're not careful, we'll wake up one day and wonder what we spent our lives doing.

I'm not saying that if you live in alignment with your values every day is going to be happy and joyful. You'll still face challenges, but the majority of the time you should be moving with a sense of peace and gratitude. Values are important because they help you make better decisions. When you have a clear picture of what's important to you, you can feel confident saying 'yes' to decisions that align with your values and 'no' to decisions that go against them. For example, a brand approaches you about a partnership. The money is good, but your values don't align with theirs, what do you do? You say 'no'. Why? Because doing work that doesn't align with your values will leave you drained and wildly unhappy and knock your confidence, which will probably diminish your ability to make money in the future.

To take another example, perhaps you've gone on a date with a very attractive person and you find out their values are very different from yours. You've not met someone this attractive in a while and you start thinking '*MaYbe I CaN ChANge them*'. No hun, say 'no' to a second date.

You have to be willing to let go of anything or anyone that wants you to hide parts of yourself so you can fit into their idea of who you are. Compromising your values means compromising your true authentic self, and that always has painful consequences.

Compromising your values means compromising your true authentic self, and that always has painful consequences.

Values are important because they also help you set boundaries in both your personal and professional life. If someone's actions consistently go against your values, you need to know when to draw the line and set a boundary. If you don't know your values, you'll let people walk over you and give people with the wrong energy too much access to your life. Let me say that again!

If you don't know your values, you'll let people walk all over you and give people with the wrong energy too much access to your life.

So let's get into how you define your values.

DEFINE YOUR VALUES

Here's a table with a list of values. Circle ten words you feel really resonate with you.

Abundance	Brilliance	Creativity
Acceptance	Calmness	Credibility
Accountability	Caring	Curiosity
Achievement	Challenge	Daring
Advancement	Charity	Decisiveness
Adventure	Cheerfulness	Dedication
Advocacy	Cleverness	Dependability
Ambition	Collaboration	Diversity
Appreciation	Commitment	Drive
Attractiveness	Community	Empathy
Autonomy	Compassion	Encouragement
Balance	Connection	Enthusiasm
Being the Best	Consistency	Ethics
Benevolence	Contribution	Excellence
Boldness	Cooperation	Expressiveness

Fairness

Family

Flexibility

Freedom

Friendships

Fun

Generosity

Grace

Growth

Happiness

Health

Honesty

Humility

Humour

Inclusiveness

Independence

Individuality

Innovation

Inspiration

Intelligence

Intuition

Joy

Kindness

Knowledge

Leadership

Learning

Love

Loyalty

Making a Difference

Mindfulness

Motivation

Open-mindedness

Optimism

Originality

Passion

Peace

Perfection

Performance

Personal
    Development

Playfulness

Popularity

Power

Preparedness

Proactive

Professionalism

Punctuality

Quality

Recognition

Relationships

Reliability

Resilience

Resourcefulness

Responsibility

Responsiveness

Risk Taking

Safety

Security

Self-control

Selflessness

Service

Simplicity

Spirituality

Stability

Success

Teamwork

Thankfulness

Thoughtfulness

Traditionalism

Tranquillity

Trustworthiness

Understanding

Uniqueness

Usefulness

Versatility

Vision

Vitality

Warmth

Wealth

Wellbeing

Wisdom

○ Next answer these questions to help you think deeper about your values and to make sure the words you've picked from the list truly resonate with you:

1. Who inspires you and why?

_____

_____

2. What do you want to stand for or be known for? If no one could see you, would you still be this way?

_____

_____

3. When have you felt fully alive? What were you doing? Why did you feel alive?

_____

_____

4. If you could make something real in the world, some sort of contribution, what would it be? *For example, if you were in a position of power, what would be the first law you would enact or change?*

_____

_____

5. What kind of person would you like to be for yourself and also for the people in your life?

_____

_____

The reasons these people, actions and ideas inspire you will indicate what you value.

○ Next, narrow your list down to your top three values:

Value 1: _____

Value 2: _____

Value 3: _____

○ What do each of these values mean to you? Write your unique definition and give each a score out of ten for how well you are honouring it and living it out:

Value 1 – Meaning: _____

_____

_____

Value 1 – Score: _____

Value 2 – Meaning: _____

_____

_____

Value 2 – Score: _____

Value 3 – Meaning: _____

_____

_____

Value 3 – Score: _____

Now that you know your top three values, you can set yourself targets to improve or maintain your score. This is intentional living at its finest and guarantees you'll keep honouring your true authentic self.

STEP 4:

UNLOCK YOUR POWER CIRCLE

Once you've articulated your strengths, passions and values, it's time to bring it all together to form your Power Circle.

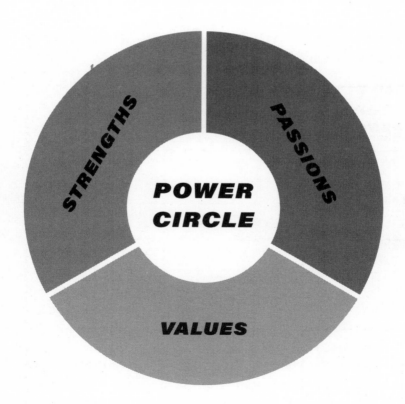

CREATE YOUR POWER CIRCLE

Write down your top strengths, passions and values from the previous exercises and begin to look for synergies between them.

TOP STRENGTHS	TOP PASSIONS	TOP VALUES

When you identify synergies in these three key areas of your life, what you'll find is that your top strengths are all you need to live out your passions and honour values.

If you can't seem to find synergies just yet, widen your scope and look at your top ten strengths, top five passions and top five values to get a broader picture.

Once you've identified your Power Circle, see how you can live from that place every day. For example, is the role you're currently in, in alignment with your Power Circle? Is there a business idea that you have? Or a community project you can volunteer on? Be as intentional as you can with it.

Use the space opposite to put down some ideas about how you can live out your Power Circle.

As you do this, you'll begin to see that:

Everything you need to win in life is already inside of you.

#CAKIMantra

It's true – everything you need to make your dreams come true is already available to you. The skills, the talents, the strengths… You already have them. And now you have come to that game-changing realisation. This is where life gets really exciting.

EVERYTHING YOU NEED TO WIN IN LIFE IS ALREADY INSIDE OF YOU

#CAKIMantra

A concept similar to the Power Circle is Ikigai. Ikigai is a Japanese concept referring to something that gives a person a sense of purpose, a reason for living. Japanese people believe that the sum of small joys in everyday life results in a more fulfilling life as a whole.

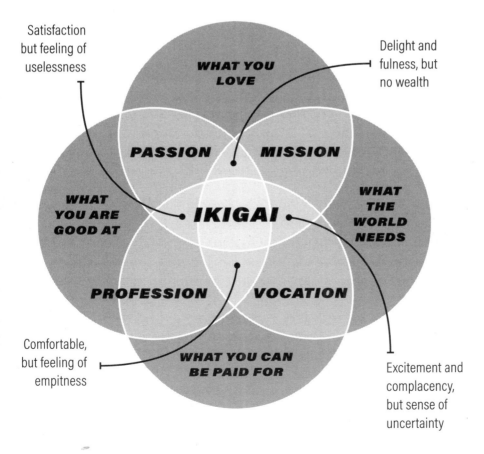

Successful people know what they are good at doing, know what they love and get about the business of doing it.

Right around the world people are discovering a purpose to their lives, a reason to be here. Oprah Winfrey famously said, 'We're all called. If you're here breathing, you have a contribution to make to our human community. The real work of your life is to figure out your function – your part in the whole – as soon as possible, and then get about the business of fulfilling it as only you can.'[1]

Successful people know what they are good at doing, know what they love and get about the business of doing it. We waste so much of our lives living for other people. We do the degree our parents want us to do, we get the job society approves of, just so we can look successful. But now it's time to stop doubting yourself. It's time to stop thinking you aren't good enough to achieve your goals. You are.

One of the reasons I'm so confident and have been able to build a successful business and impact so many lives isn't because I'm special. It's because I'm strategic. I figured out this magic equation in my early twenties and got into alignment with my Power Circle. My business is literally built at the intersection of my strengths, passions and values, and so every day when I show up, I'm living from a place of strength and doing what sets my heart on fire. Becoming an entrepreneur is hard: if you want to be in it for the long run and seriously thrive make sure you're in alignment with your Power Circle.

Here's what my winning equation looks like:

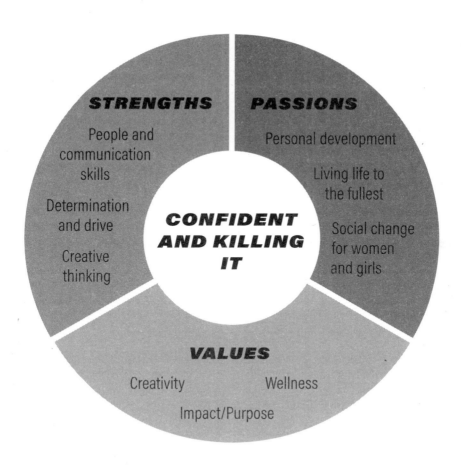

CONFIDENT AND KILLING IT IN ACTION

Tochi, a dear friend and client of mine who has now become a member of the Confident and Killing It team, had a huge wake-up moment in our Power Circle coaching session.

In 2020 she was working for a law firm in New York and, in her words, 'following the path my parents laid out for me that would make me a good example for my younger siblings and also make them proud'. However, when we looked at the synergies between her top strengths, passions and values, everything was demonstrating that she should be following a career that drew on her love and talent for yoga and wellness.

Deep down she always knew she wanted to be a wellness entrepreneur, but she questioned her ability to make it happen and succeed at it. Identifying her Power Circle was exactly the wake-up call she needed to be confident and pursue her dream:

Top Strengths	Top Passions	Top Values
Positive energy.	Yoga, meditation, wellness and beauty.	Growth.
Leadership and communication skills.	Social impact.	Community.
Having a creative eye.	Entrepreneurship.	Being fearless.

As you can see, there is so much synergy between those three areas, she already has everything she needs to be a good entrepreneur. Everything she needs to be impactful in the wellness industry is already inside her.

After that session she realised the best way to set an example for her siblings was not to follow the traditional career path her parents expected of her, but actually to live her life in alignment with strengths, passions and values. By suppressing her fulfilment and living under the weight of fear and others' expectations, she was actually doing a disservice to the people she wanted to serve the most – her loved ones. As we reflected on that session together, she went on to say, 'It was emotional for me because I realised that by living in my authenticity and truth I would be setting a much better example for my siblings and creating space for a more honest relationship with my parents. The best thing I could do for myself and for them was to actually live in my authenticity and power.'

How beautiful is that? Well I'm happy to share that after our coaching sessions, Tochi started putting plans in place to leave the job that wasn't in alignment with her Power Circle and she's now officially a full-time yoga instructor and wellness entrepreneur!

STEP 5:

CREATE YOUR PURPOSE

Now that you've warmed up to the idea of living from your Power Circle, it's time to think about how it can be used for something bigger than yourself, aka your purpose. Your Power Circle isn't meant just for you, it's meant for you and to be shared with the world so we can make that world a better place. Purpose is about being in the service of something bigger than yourself, and you can create your own purpose through your Power Circle. Notice I said *create* purpose and not 'find', 'discover', 'pray for', etc. No one is born knowing their purpose; purpose is something you create as you live authentically and intentionally. It isn't an end goal, or something that just drops down from heaven, it's more of a journey. It's active. It's a daily practice.

No one is born knowing their purpose; purpose is something you create as you live authentically and intentionally.

I would have never known what I was capable of building with Confident and Killing It had I not been intentional about finding my flow. I quit my job at the engineering company to get a job working in social impact for Girl Effect, an NGO that uses media, technology and content to empower teenage girls living in developing countries. I also started making one-minute videos on Instagram using my communication skills to inspire women and girls to love themselves. The more I operated from my Power Circle and used it for something bigger than myself, the more clarity and confirmation I got on the purpose of my life. So if you're unsure about what your purpose is, follow the path where your strengths, passions and values align.

A word of caution: being in the service of something bigger than yourself doesn't mean losing or neglecting yourself in order to serve the world, your family or your partner. Breaking yourself into pieces in order to serve others is *not* your purpose. You must always fill your cup up first and serve the world from your overflow, not from an empty cup. It's not selfish. Your worth is not based on your ability to help people. Your worth is tied to your mere existence. So, I like to see purpose as giving a part of my own greatness as a gift to the world. I'm not giving all of myself so I'm left with nothing. I'm sharing a part of my magic so you can enjoy and experience it too!

It's also important to acknowledge that not everyone wants to be seen as 'inspiring' or a role model. You might prefer to live low key and serve behind the scenes. That's OK too! Just make sure you're not hiding your gifts under the guise of being 'humble'.

I want to end this chapter with one single message:

AUTOPILOT AIN'T CUTE.

You owe it to yourself to be awake to your own life, know what sets you apart, know what you are good at doing and realise that everything you need to win in life is already within you. Your starting place is good enough, but as you go through each moment, day and season, you're evolving and getting closer and closer to your truest, most beautiful authentic self, and you're doing that until your last days. So, keep an open mind as you read this book and begin to discover new parts of yourself. The more you know and accept your authentic self, the more you'll know and accept your sense of worth and personal power. On one hand, you'll be less likely to let fear and the naysayers get in your way, because deep down you'll know who you are and what you deserve. And on the other hand, you'll be more likely to believe in your capability to turn your ideas into action, and that's exactly what confidence is about.

In the next chapter we're going to look at how you can begin to challenge and let go of old limiting narratives and create beautiful, empowering ones. I'm right here with you and I'm excited for you as we continue to get Confident and Killing It.

2

GETTING SASSY WITH THE MEAN GIRL IN YOUR MIND

As you get more intentional about being your authentic self and living from your Power Circle, your mind will often feel like a battlefield. Your newfound confidence and power will be in a tussle with your old thoughts and behaviours that have been running the show. One of the biggest confidence killers you'll come up against is the negative voice in your head. I call mine 'the Mean Girl', and that's the name I'm going to use here. If you've got another name for yours, feel free to use that. Whatever her name, you'll know her. She's that voice in between your ears that tells you you're not good enough, not smart enough and/or not pretty enough. She tends to show up before really important moments, such as when you want to speak up in a meeting or put yourself forward for an opportunity. She's always pointing out how everyone is ahead of you in life and you're not doing enough. She's also super-critical of everything you do. 'That was stupid. Why did you say that?' 'OMG, did you really type that out in an email and send it? *So* embarrassing.' 'You haven't worked hard enough, you don't deserve to have a rest. You're not even successful yet!'

The Mean Girl says she's there to protect you, but all she ends up doing is stressing you out and making you doubt yourself. She's the first to let you know you're not qualified enough for that job or that you really have no idea what you're doing and you're going to be exposed as the imposter you truly are. Even as I write these pages, my Mean Girl is asking me to rethink, because since when did I have the intellect to write a whole book?

I'm pretty sure you can relate to everything I've just said. If you can't, well, how does it feel to be God's favourite? For us regular humans, our mind is a battlefield.

Your mind is like a battlefield of conflicting forces. It usually works against you, but you can program it to work for you.

#CAKIMantra

It may feel as though the negativity is winning, but not anymore, baby girl, we're about to change that.

WHY ARE OUR MINDS SO NEGATIVE?

OK, it seems that our negative thoughts have so much power over us because of a thing called negativity bias. This is because negative events have more of an impact on our brains than positive ones. Negativity bias was useful earlier in human history when we needed to be constantly on the lookout for what could go wrong so we could stay safe and survive. Being aware of threats was literally a matter of life and death. While those historic threats don't exist in today's world and society has evolved a lot, our brain really hasn't evolved that much. It still scans our environment for danger and is often jumping into the future, reaching wild conclusions and, more often than not, the worst possible outcome. We remember criticism more than we do praise, we remember embarrassing situations more easily

YOUR MIND IS LIKE A BATTLEFIELD OF CONFLICTING FORCES.

IT USUALLY WORKS AGAINST YOU, BUT YOU CAN PROGRAM IT TO WORK FOR YOU.

#CAKIMantra

than we do moments where we've been proud of ourselves, all so we never repeat those negative moments again. Our brain's job is to keep us alive, so anything that feels embarrassing, shameful, hurtful or like a near-death experience is locked into our memory to prevent it from happening again.

And then to further cement the negativity, we also experience a phenomenon called confirmation bias, whereby whenever we have a belief, our brain looks for evidence to confirm that belief. So if we have a negative thought about ourselves, for example 'I'm bad with money', our brain will look for evidence to confirm this, like that time we ordered takeaway every day of the week.

Our mind also gets really negative when we aren't living in alignment with our Power Circle and our true authentic selves. When I was stuck in a job I hated, I would show up every day thinking, 'I hate this job, I'm terrible at this, no one likes me, I really don't care about any of this.' That constant negativity was the perfect place for my Mean Girl to thrive and for depression to kick in. If you're not honouring your strengths, passions and values, it means you're doing the opposite – you're living from your limitations, you're not feeling alive and you're not doing

When you feel unfulfilled, you begin to feel you're not in control of your life and you let the Mean Girl kick your ass all the time.

what matters to you. It's an absolute confidence killer. This is why the work you did to unlock your Power Circle in the last chapter was so important. When you feel unfulfilled, you begin to feel you're not in control of your life and you let the Mean Girl kick your ass all the time.

HOW TO TAP INTO THE POWER OF YOUR MIND

Do you know you can actually *reprogram your mind* to be less negative and more positive? You don't have to live in bondage. You, yes, you reading this book right now, can turn down the volume of the Mean Girl and turn up the volume of your Inner Cheerleader.

Your Inner Cheerleader is a real ally. It can be a song, a person you admire, your grandmother's voice or the positive voice in your head. Whenever I feel nervous, I find the nearest toilet and secretly dance to Beyoncé; she's my ally when I need to channel some bold energy. Or, on days, when I need to feel more grounded and connect with my intuition, I lean into Oprah's wisdom (hence my tagline: 'If Beyoncé and Oprah had a baby, it would be me.')

Your ability to reprogram your mind is thanks to your brain's 'neuroplasticity'.[1] Science has confirmed that the brain is a dynamic organ and has the capacity to be shaped, trained and influenced in response to new information and life experiences. It has the ability to be mentally flexible and adapt to change over time by creating new neurons and connections that lead to new behaviours. This completely challenges the excuses that people often give for not changing: 'I'm stuck in my ways' or 'It's just the way I am.' But you can be different! Change isn't easy, but it is always possible with intentionality and practice.

Great examples of neuroplasticity have been seen in the brain's ability to learn new things like languages as well as heal and rebuild itself following damage like strokes and traumatic brain injuries. In 1996 Dr Jill Bolte Taylor, a Harvard-trained brain researcher, experienced a severe stroke that caused her to lose the ability to walk, talk, read, write or recall any of her life. It took eight years for her to rebuild her brain and recover all her physical, emotional, and thinking abilities, but she did it, and now she is the author of two *New York Times* bestselling books, and her TED talk, 'My Stroke of Insight', has been watched 28 million times![2] This is the power of neuroplasticity.

The biggest, most life-changing realisation of my twenties was understanding the power of my mind and how to program it for success. In this chapter I'm going to show you how to do the same in a very practical way.

YOU BECOME
WHAT YOU BELIEVE

It's scientifically proven that our thoughts influence our feelings and our feelings influence the actions we take. What we believe about ourselves is the foundation for who we become. When we believe we are a nice person, we do nice things for other people. When we believe we are creative, we do creative things. So deciding to believe positive and truthful things about ourselves is fundamental to living a positive and fulfilled life.

As you learned earlier, our beliefs come from external and internal sources. Some we absorb from childhood and the world around us and others we create ourselves, based on our experiences, feelings and the meaning we give to them.

Our thoughts become beliefs when we think *and* act in accordance with them over and over again. So let's say one day I think I'm a failure. If I begin to dwell on it and act like a failure, I'll develop a new belief about myself. When I believe I'm a failure, I'll feel terrible, will most likely be anxious about my future, won't try new things and will disqualify myself from opportunities, because I'm a failure, so what's the point? All of this *guarantees* failure.

Believe you're worthy of your dreams coming true and you'll go after them with relentless passion.

On the other hand, let's say I do a good presentation at work and the thought pops into my head that I have good people and communication skills. If I reflect on the presentation and replay all the moments that went really well, I'll begin to see myself as someone with good people and communication skills who can deliver good presentations. I'll start feeling more confident when it comes to public speaking and I'll put myself up for more opportunities.

As you can see, whatever you believe is what you respond to. Believe you're bad with people and social situations, and you'll develop social anxiety. Believe you're worthy of your dreams coming true and you'll go after them with relentless passion. Your beliefs either sabotage you or empower you. They harm you or they heal you. It's so important to be fully awake to how your mind works and what you personally believe about yourself.

HOW TO WIN THE BATTLE IN YOUR MIND

Now a lot of us want to be more positive and we really do try, but we just get attacked by unsolicited negative thoughts all the time. It's just our Mean Girl doing what she does best. What can we do about her?

Not every single thought about yourself is the truth about who you are.

We can't always control what thoughts pop into our head, but we can control whether a negative thought is repeated so much it turns into a limiting belief. If it does, it's going to require some awareness to first identify the limiting belief and then break the pattern. This chapter will give you some insight into what some of your limiting beliefs could be and how you can let go of them. I really wish I'd known this earlier, but now I do, and I'm sharing it with you, so you know too.

Not every single thought about yourself is the truth about who you are. Some are lies with a sprinkle of truth, some are straight-out lies and some are actually the truth. It is your job to filter them and decide which ones you're going to keep as beliefs and which ones you're going to label as rubbish and bin. Try viewing your thoughts as objects floating past you, you can stop and observe them or you can just let them pass.

Now you might be thinking, 'Tiwa, you don't understand – my Mean Girl is *mean*. Like worse than Regina George type of mean. She's been this way my whole life. I don't think she'll ever go away.'

First, I want you to know I totally resonate with what you may be thinking and any doubts you might be having. I was the same seven years ago before I started my journey towards becoming Confident and Killing It. However, the goal is *not* for the Mean

Girl to disappear forever. Unfortunately, she can't be annihilated. **Confidence is not the absence of negative thoughts or self-doubt**. Confidence is not feeling happy and clappy all the time. Confidence is *not* perfection. I would be lying if I said I had the magic equation to get rid of self-doubt forever. I don't. But I do know that confidence is about having a deep belief in yourself and your abilities. It's about learning to move past the fear and insecurity and *bet* on yourself. It's about understanding that even when you don't know what the future holds, you believe that you are worthy of living an abundant life, a life you truly desire and a life you will take action on.

So, as I said, the goal is not to get rid of the Mean Girl forever. A little bit of self-doubt actually keeps us grounded, because it forces us to reflect, slow down and acknowledge our imperfections. So it's not all bad news, you just need to learn to reprogram your mind, so your default is no longer negativity, self-doubt and fear, but confidence, positivity, self-worth, abundance, joy, peace, excitement, passion and all the other good stuff.

At 21, I made the life-changing decision that my default would no longer be allowing my Mean Girl to bash me but instead I would wake up every day and *choose love*, because loving yourself is something you *choose* to do, not something you're born knowing how to do.

Confidence is not the absence of negative thoughts or self-doubt.

So, I would look in the mirror every day and say, '*Tiwa, I. Love. You.*' Every single day, even when I didn't feel like it, I still said it, because I wanted to send a loud and clear message to my Mean Girl that she no longer had power over me and that regardless of my emotions, as a bare minimum I would always love myself. This is something I recommend you do too. You may look in the mirror every day, but do you really look into your eyes and see yourself and appreciate what's there? Looking into your eyes and thinking nice things about yourself is a quick self-care practice you can tag on at the end of your morning skin-care routine.

Now, this battle we're fighting isn't easy. It's hard, but as author and activist Glennon Doyle says, 'Life is hard but we can do hard things.' You might not believe it's possible for you, but I believe it is, and I believe in you. You might not love yourself, but I love you. You might not see your greatness, but I see it. I see it all. And I want nothing more in life than to see you winning. I want nothing more in life than to see you make your mind work for you rather than against you. So, let's put the Mean Girl in her place.

In 2018, I was hosting one of my Confident and Killing It events in London. There were about fifty women in the room who had bought tickets to come and hear me speak. The event was called 'Own Your Story' and was about learning to know your truth, speak your truth and celebrate your truth. As I was speaking, I was met with a sea of faces looking intently, taking notes and processing all that I was saying. At that moment, my Mean Girl showed up and whispered, 'Look at all their faces. They're bored. You need to shut up right now. You need to end this event. You've been talking for too long. They don't care, they just want to go home. Shut up, shut up, shut uuuuup.'

Bear in mind, all of this was happening as I was standing in front of fifty women, talking to them about confidence. This was *not* the time for this BS. In that moment I had two choices, choices which are available to all of us. I could listen to my Mean Girl (and end the event early) *or* I could ask myself some questions to confirm the validity of what she was saying. I did that using the Negative Thought Detector. Here's how it works.

NEGATIVE THOUGHT DETECTOR

QUESTION 1:

'IS THIS 100 PER CENT FACT OR AM I MAKING AN ASSUMPTION?'

The first step I took was to get inquisitive. I asked myself, 'Is it 100 per cent fact that people are bored or am I making an assumption?' How accurate is this thought? What evidence did I have to prove that people were actually bored and wanted to go home? I had none. I couldn't read their minds, so I had no idea what they were actually thinking and no one was sneaking out the back door. I was making an assumption. A negative one at that, and one that wasn't serving me in any way.

If your thought is a fact, then fine, focus on what you can control and leave what you don't have the power to change. For example, if people were actually bored, I would have probably had a quick fifteen-minute interval, played some music, got everyone moving their body and passed around some snacks! Then I would have had a quick debrief with my team to see if they had any opinions on what was missing, I'd take their feedback on board then get back into it.

However, if your thought is an assumption, then it can be changed. In *Why Has Nobody Told Me This Before?* therapist Dr Julie Smith says a big step towards taking the power out of negative thoughts is to notice when they appear and understand them for what they are. Let's look at a few different types of thought biases we all experience:

○ **Mind reading** – making assumptions about what others are thinking. For example assuming everyone was bored at my event.

○ **Overgeneralising** – taking what happened in one experience and assuming it's the same for all future or past experiences. For example one piece of negative feedback about your work means all your work is now terrible.

○ **Musts and shoulds** – having unrealistic expectations and putting pressure on yourself to be, look or feel a certain way and then assuming you're a failure when you don't measure up.

○ **Catastrophising** – always assuming the worst possible outcome without considering possibilities that are more likely and more realistic.

○ **Emotional reasoning** – thinking if you feel a certain way about an event then it must be true. How many times have you felt you messed up an interview so badly only to get a call that you got the place. Feelings aren't facts, more on that in the next section.

○ **Black or white thinking** – thinking in absolute extremes, like: if I'm not pretty, then I'm ugly. If I'm not 100 per cent good at it then I'm terrible. It's all or nothing.

Dwelling on these types of thoughts and taking them as the absolute truth will keep us in a low mood and get us into trouble later down the line. If your default is to assume the worst of people and yourself as a safety mechanism, really pay attention to this as most of your assumptions may end up being inaccurate.

QUESTION 2:

'WOULD I EVER SAY THIS TO A FRIEND?'

We are so nice and loving to our friends and family, but so mean and critical to ourselves.

Would you ever say this to a friend?

○ 'Don't speak up, you might say something stupid.'

○ 'Why are you so awkward with people? Honestly, you're so cringe.'

○ 'Everyone is low-key looking, judging you. Btw, this was a very bad outfit choice.'

○ 'Yup, I knew you were going to mess this up. They're going to find out you have no idea what you're doing. You should quit ASAP.'

○ 'Mmmhh, you don't really look good today. Delete that picture and don't keep trying.'

You would *never, ever, ever* say these things to your best friend, would you?!

Well, listen up, you are your own best friend. So give yourself some grace and kindness too. If you would never say something out loud to a friend, don't say it to yourself either. You're just as worthy of the love and encouragement you give other people, OK? OK!

Back to when I was freaking out internally. In that moment, I caught a glimpse of my friend Leanne, who was sitting in the front row smiling at me. I tried to imagine what she would say to me. She's one of the most supportive people ever and I knew she would probably say something like: 'Tee, you're Killing It. Did you see the way those girls were looking up at you? Honestly I'm so proud of you, man. I remember when you started in Oxford and look at you now!'

So the thought that I was doing a bad job and everyone was bored contradicted my answer to this second question. I would never say that to a friend. If you find yourself thinking these kinds of thoughts, check whether you'd be happy to say them to someone else.

QUESTION 3:

'DOES THIS THOUGHT SABOTAGE ME OR EMPOWER ME?'

On to the final step. Thinking people were bored and wanted to go home in the middle of my event definitely wasn't empowering. If I'd listened to my Mean Girl, I would have given up halfway through and not given the women in attendance the full experience they paid for. I mean, the goody bags hadn't even come out yet!

Here's my rule of thumb:

**If a thought sabotages you, *bin it.*
If a thought empowers you, *run with it.***

#CAKIMantra

Sing it with me, ladies:

If it sabotages you, *bin it*. If it empowers you, *run with it*.
If it sabotages you, *bin it*. If it empowers you, *run with it*.
If it sabotages you, *bin it*. If it empowers you, *run with it*.

Sabotaging thoughts belong in the bin, the trash, *la poubelle, la basura*, whatever you call it. They keep you stuck in a life you don't want. They make you shrink and want to give up. Empowering thoughts elevate you. They encourage you to keep moving forward and most of all, they are who you really are.

Sabotaging thoughts belong in the bin.

IF A THOUGHT SABOTAGES YOU, *BIN IT.*

IF A THOUGHT EMPOWERS YOU, *RUN WITH IT.*

#CAKIMantra

So, when you question what your Mean Girl is telling you and you can see that it's an assumption, that you would never say that to a friend and that it's sabotaging you, pay it less attention and *shift your focus* to something more empowering, realistic and truthful *based on your strengths*. Don't fake the positivity but instead take a moment to explore a more helpful perspective.

The moment I gave myself permission to make a different choice – a choice that is available to all of us – I activated my Inner Cheerleader and a positive and a powerful voice in my head kicked in: 'Fifty women have paid to come and hear me speak. They are not bored. I have flown all over the world to speak to women and girls. Remember the time I got invited to the Oprah Winfrey Leadership Academy to speak? Or the time my first event sold out in two days with 200 sign-ups? Because I'm a captivating, inspiring and powerful speaker. Communication is one of my key strengths. People constantly tell me how powerful my words are and how those words have changed their life, so *you* had better shut up and get to the back of the line with your negative ass energy.'

Ding, ding, ding! Tiwa 1 – 0 Mean Girl

And that, ladies, is how you win the battle against the Mean Girl. You can't just let her stroll into your mind, grab a glass of wine and some popcorn and talk rubbish. No, ma'am. You've got to come at her with some heat so she knows who runs things around here. Did you notice my Cheerleader didn't just say, 'Oh, Tiwa's a nice girl, please stop being mean to her, please.' *No, she came with the receipts*. She came with hardcore facts that were true and could not be contested.

Your Inner Cheerleader isn't only for big moments. They're an ally that's there to help you in every moment of your life.

Sharon, an Australian member of the Confident and Killing It Academy, posted this lovely message about when she tackled her Mean Girl:

'I had been following an entrepreneur on Instagram for quite some time and did one of her workshops last year. One evening at the end of Nov., she posted an IG story looking for ongoing help within her business. I initially hesitated because I "didn't feel ready", didn't think I'd tick all the boxes of what she needed and she's a dream client, so the thought of approaching her made me nervous.

'First thing I did which I learnt from coaching with Tiwa was to reframe my thought, I switched "what if I'm not who she wants to work with?" to "what if I'm exactly who she needs?" Next, I channelled my mum's fearless energy. Whilst working full time ten years ago, she went back to further her education and got a qualification in fashion textiles and merchandising, which involved using a lot of digital design tools she had never used before. She also started singing lessons and picked up Spanish and French, all at the age of 60! If she's not letting fear get in the way of her dreams at that age, then why should I? I bit *the bullet and responded. Well, I'm rapt to say that after six months of no work and being "wishy washy" with my life plans, I finished 2021 with my first client (literally, contract signed Dec. 31) in my new business! I'm hitting the ground running in January as we officially begin working together tomorrow and I haven't been this excited in a long time! Thank you, Tiwa, for creating this academy.'*

In this situation Sharon knew that her thoughts were sabotaging her, so she binned them, chose a more empowering thought with the help of her mum's fearless energy as her Ally and then followed through with action.

Getting sassy with the Mean Girl in your mind isn't about reciting overly positive 'You go, girl' affirmations that you got off Google. This is about going deeper to really know and articulate your strengths and the positive things about you. Using your 'I am…' strength affirmations from Chapter 1 for example: 'I am… because… A time when I showed this was when…' is a powerful way to challenge the Mean Girl, because it is rooted in the truth of who you are with real-life evidence to back you up.

Another way to visualise getting sassy with the Mean Girl is imagine you're in a court case between you and your imposter syndrome. Your imposter syndrome is trying to throw you in jail because it believes you're a fraud and you need to defend yourself.

The prosecutors have all the evidence and examples of how you're a fraud because of the reasons we previously talked about, like negativity bias and our brain's hyper-awareness of moments when we've felt shame, failure or embarrassment.

Now imagine your lawyer strolling into the courtroom late with no paperwork, holding a Margarita and saying to the judge and jury, 'Guysss, c'mmon, she's a great gal. She's not a fraud. Trust me. Just give her a chance. I promise she's a good person. #positivevibesonly.'

Who do you think is going to win that case?

Most likely the prosecutors who have the receipts and better evidence. So, if you want to win the case against your Mean Girl, you have to come up with an even more compelling argument as to why you are not a fraud. You have to go digging for evidence of your wins and accomplishments. As we discovered in Chapter 1, you need to know your strengths, why they belong to you and when you have displayed them, so you have all the evidence you need to win the battle in your mind.

Confidence is a practice. It's about setting yourself up for success. No one shows up to a fight half asleep. You need to be fully awake with a winning strategy to hand. Think of building your confidence in the same way.

If you want to win the case against your Mean Girl, you have to come up with an even more compelling argument as to why you are not a fraud.

Once you've articulated your strengths, they become the empowering language you use to get sassy with the Mean Girl. Whenever she shows up with her lies and false accusations, you kill those lies with the truth of who you really are.

The Negative Thought Detector is a quick and practical way to deal with negative thoughts on the spot when you don't have time for deep introspective thinking and feeling. However, for real confidence and to let go of more ingrained limiting beliefs, you'll need a lot of practice and space to go deeper into how to manage and process not just your thoughts, but your emotions and actions too.

RIDING THE WAVE OF YOUR EMOTIONS

Emotions, emotions, emotions. I know some of you already want to skip the next few pages because... emotions? 'Ewww, don't do those.'

That was me too. In my mind I was a *strong independent woman*, so anything that didn't align with that had to be buried. I thought happiness, success and joy were for feeling, and pain, heartbreak and disappointment were for fixing, burying or ignoring. When I started my life-coaching training, though, I soon learned that being human isn't about only feeling happiness and ignoring everything else, being human is about feeling *all* your emotions. Emotions aren't 'good' or 'bad', they're neutral. They're just energy in motion.

E - M - O - T - I - O - N - S = energy in motion

Emotions flow in and they flow out. We experience a whole wave of emotions every day, and that isn't a bad thing. It's the meaning we give to our emotions that makes us embrace them or avoid them. The worst thing we can do for our growth is to only expect 'positive' emotions every day of our life, because if our goal is only to be happy then we are going to limit the richness of our life. There is often meaning and beauty in the pain.

I remember watching an episode of Oprah's *Super Soul Sunday* where she mentioned that pain was like a knock on your door. 'When you open the door and see who's there,' she said, 'don't shut it straight away, welcome it in and ask it, "What are you here to teach me?" Don't fight your pain. Invite it in and sit with it for a bit.'

Now you might be thinking, 'This sounds dumb. Why on Earth would I want to invite pain into my life? Hellooo, I'm trying to be trauma free.' Yes, I know it sounds a bit crazy, but you can't control everything that happens to you in life. You can control how you respond, but you can't control every single occurrence. So there will be pain you can avoid by making smart decisions, like setting boundaries with toxic people, for example. But there will be pain that arrives without an invitation. It barges right in and even if you run into your room, lock the door and hide under your bed, the pain whips up a storm in your house until you eventually have to come out. So don't run from it, sit with

Emotions aren't 'good' or 'bad', they're neutral. They're just energy in motion.

it. Yes, it's going to be hard, yes, it's going to be uncomfortable, but in the end it will be worth it. Why? Because purpose can be created from pain.

I'm not saying 'EVerYThInG HapPEns FoR a ReASOn' because sometimes bad things happen to good people who don't deserve it at all! Adversity can lead to positive growth, but that doesn't mean we have to be *grateful* that a horrible experience happened. What I'm saying here is you might have found yourself in a situation that you thought would totally break you, but it didn't, and now your awareness of yourself and what you believe you can handle has grown. There might also be someone out there going through the same struggles as you did and they think they're alone, they think they can't get through it, but then they hear your story, they see you waving from out the other side, and they get back up again and keep going. They see that you've done it, so now they know they can do it too. That's one way I believe we can find meaning in pain.

CONFIDENT AND KILLING IT IN ACTION

My friend Mena is a perfect example of someone I've seen create purpose from pain. After a very close cousin of hers died of cancer, she went through a period of depression. She was 28 at the time, living with her parents and struggling to find a job, despite being very qualified. The weight of needing to have her life all figured out while trying to grieve for her cousin was crippling.

From this pain came an idea for a community: the L8 Bloomers. One night at 2 a.m. she just thought, 'How amazing would it be to create a platform where we can share this real-life journey unashamedly? Adulting in the 21st century is hard, and it doesn't help when everyone is pretending to be perfect. The L8 Bloomers would be a community of millennials sharing personal stories of life unfiltered and beyond social constructs and expectations.' She calls it the REAL (highlight) Reel.

Opening up about her pain, going to therapy, leaning into the light and getting life-coach training has led to a series of authentic and vulnerable conversations that have freed many people from the weight of society's expectations.

Adversity is not a precursor for growth but, when combined with proper support mechanisms like a growth mindset, which we'll look at in the next chapter, therapy and coaching, it can make you stronger by pushing you to think differently and be more resourceful and resilient when future challenges occur.

So how do you sit with pain? It's time for some practical application with the 3As.

THE 3AS

When things go wrong, don't beat yourself up about it or dwell on it for so long that it spills into other areas of your life, try these steps instead:

1. *Acknowledge* how you're feeling

2. *Articulate* what you're feeling

3. *Allow* yourself to move forward

STEP 1:

ACKNOWLEDGE HOW YOU'RE FEELING

This is simply accepting the fact that you feel a bit shit. It's not a personal failure to admit this. In fact, you can scream it out loud right now if that's how you feel. I'm not judging you. I scream into my pillow sometimes. Acknowledgement is so important, because you can't process something if you don't even acknowledge it exists. A lot of people avoid going to therapy because they can't bear the thought of actually acknowledging what has happened to them. But 'to overcome it, we have to face it' – there's no other way through.

As a child who grew up in a Christian home, I thought that if I believed in God, loved people and obeyed my parents, then everything would go exactly how I planned, right?

Wrong.

Life is a rollercoaster not a straight path. It goes up and down, fast and slow, and sometimes it feels like you're even spinning upside down. It's all part of what being human means. Make peace with it and don't judge yourself. No one is meant to feel 100 per cent, 100 per cent of the time.

Only focusing on positive emotions and avoiding or rejecting anything negative is not a realistic or healthy way to live and is actually what we now describe as 'toxic positivity'. So, instead of saying things like 'Always look on the bright side' to a friend who's dealing with disappointment, try, 'It can be difficult to see the good in this situation, but we'll make sense of what we can.' Instead of trying to make yourself feel better by comparing your sad situation to someone who 'has it worse', validate your own emotions by embracing your authentic human experience. Good mental health isn't perfect mental health. Emotions are complex and we never just feel one way anyway. We can be an optimistic and positive person while also acknowledging our hurt, anger or fear.

Start to notice your natural emotional pattern so you don't get surprised by your mood swings. For example, after an amazing International Women's Day month in March where I was booked, busy and smashing glass ceilings, I woke up one day with an overwhelming amount of sadness. My chest was heavy, I felt like crying, I had no energy in me, and no, it wasn't my period. I don't know what it was, but boy, was I sad. I started seeing a pattern: after I do something really big with next-level energy, passion and focus,

I get thrown into a sad state where I just feel numb for weeks. When we're in a low mood, our first response is often to think 'something is wrong with me'; however, thinking that can make us feel helpless. In reality our low mood is probably from an unmet need or just our natural emotional wave, so instead of thinking you're broken, ask yourself: 'Which need am I not meeting?' and take it from there.

Look out for your own emotional patterns. You can keep a journal and track your moods, or there's an app called Moody I love that allows you to do this in a fun and modern way. Being more self-aware allows you to be proactive about your wellbeing instead of feeling you're constantly fighting fires.

STEP 2:

ARTICULATE WHAT YOU'RE FEELING

Once you've acknowledged that you're in a funk, start to find the words to express what you're feeling. Get it out through speaking to someone about it or journaling. There are so many studies on the power of journaling. It's been shown to validate our emotions and connect us to what's real, it's been used to cure different disorders, and it's also a fantastic way to release difficult emotions and gather insights about what our pain and discomfort mean. A 2005 study by the University of Cambridge showed that writing about traumatic, stressful or emotional events results in improvements in both physical and psychological health.[3] Expressive writing can clear your mind's worries and free up resources in your brain that could be put to use on other tasks. It can lead to better sleep, a stronger immune system and more self-confidence.[4] James W. Pennebaker, a social psychologist at the University of Texas who is considered the pioneer of writing therapy, has also stated that labelling emotions and acknowledging traumatic events – both natural outcomes of journaling – have a positive effect on people.[5] Here's a tool called the Wheel of Emotions to help you put a name to what you're feeling:

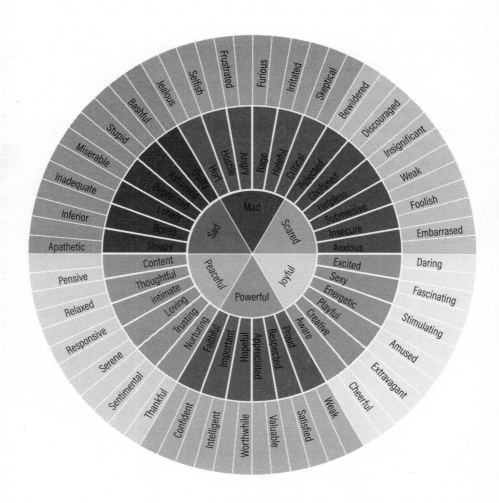

There's no right or wrong way to journal, you have full creative liberty and expression, but if you don't know where to start, here are a few ways:

✨ FREE FLOW

Sit down, get still, breathe deeply, *feel*, then let it all out.

○   Where in your body are you feeling emotional pain?

○   What's going on in your mind?

○   What's going on in your environment?

Just dump of all the different emotions you're feeling and worries you're having. Write without judgement. Write like you're breaking up with your ex. Just keep going, and if an intrusive thought pops in, welcome it and write it down too.

Some people will rip it all up when they're done, others will go back to further analyse why they're feeling a certain way. Experiment and do what works best for you.

✦ 'I RELEASE AND I WELCOME'

○ Make a list of all the things inside you that feel heavy and that you want to release.

○ Then make a list of all the things you want to welcome.

Here's a snippet from my diary from May 2021:

I release negativity.

I release stiffness.

I release heaviness.

I release insecurity.

I release fear.

I release overwhelm.

I release numbness.

I release pain.

I welcome freedom.

I welcome love.

I welcome friendship.

I welcome peace.

I welcome progress.

I welcome wisdom.

I welcome determination.

I welcome compassion.

○   Once you've finished, meditate on the things you're welcoming and visualise yourself feeling those positive emotions. Creating images of these positive and soothing associations can help release stress, regulate your emotions and boost your energy. It can also provide an amazing source of hope and inspiration when you're feeling down. Moving your body is also essential to releasing heavy emotions. I often do Yoga With Adrienne's YouTube tutorial for Anxiety and Stress or attend a kickboxing class.

✨ EXPLORING A MEMORY

Think about an experience or memory that brings up painful emotions and then answer these questions:

○   What thoughts did you have about this experience and what it meant to you?

○   What negative emotions surface most often around it (like anxiety, shame or guilt)?

○   How did you respond to the emotional pain? How were actions helpful and unhelpful to you?

○   In what ways is the emotional pain a result of the unrealistic demands you put on yourself, others and the world around you?

If journaling still isn't your thing and you prefer to speak to people, make sure you are speaking to someone you trust. Not everyone can handle your energy when you're in a low place and it's also not fair to continuously dump your pain on your friends and family instead of going to see a proper professional about it. My rule of thumb is if you're stuck in the odd rut here and there, be vulnerable and open up to someone you respect and trust. If it's something heavy that keeps coming up for you over and over again, then speak to a therapist or coach about it so you can learn the right techniques to finally heal and grow through it.

STEP 3:

ALLOW YOURSELF TO MOVE FORWARD

The great thing about rollercoasters is, like life, no matter how crazy or scary the ride is, it keeps moving forward until it reaches the finish line. It never ends while you're mid-air screaming for your life. No matter how turbulent it is, you always reach the end. In the same way, when you feel that life is taking you on a wild ride, remember it doesn't end that way. Rest when you need to, ask for help when you need to, and then get back up and give yourself permission to move forward. Forgive yourself, forgive others and try your best to focus on how you would rather feel, because a new and stronger you will emerge. A lot of us want to be resilient, but we don't want to go through the tough situations that actually cultivate resilience and strength. So, accept your 'negative' emotions as an opportunity to build resilience. The key is not to get stuck in them.

To start moving forward when you've been in a rut, get intentional about building your positive emotions back up. The 'P' in the

PERMA model – the five pillars of wellbeing – stands for 'Positive Emotions'. Reports show that when we feel good, we perform better at work and study; positive emotions boost our physical health; they strengthen our relationships and inspire us to be creative, take charge and look to the future with optimism and hope. Here are some things to try:

✨ MINDFULNESS MEDITATION

Practising mindfulness involves being in the present moment without worry and regret. When you feel regret about your past, you feel depressed; when you worry about your future, you feel anxious. Grounding yourself in the present moment by observing your thoughts, feelings and sensations without judgement does wonders for your mental and emotional health.

Box breathing is my favourite way of doing it:

○ Use your index finger to hold one nostril down.

○ Breathe in the other nostril for four seconds.

○ Hold your breath for four seconds.

○ Switch your fingers and breathe out of your other nostril for four seconds.

○ Hold your breath again for four seconds.

○ And repeat.

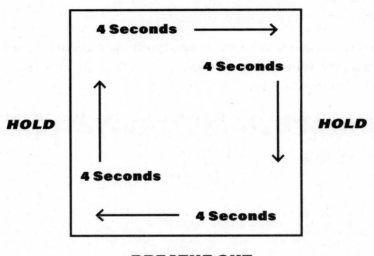

✦ GET INTENTIONAL ABOUT WHAT BRINGS YOU JOY

Make a list of all the things you love doing, then schedule in time in your calendar to do one of them every day. This will ensure any unmet needs that may be causing your low mood are prioritised.

For starters, you can find joy in special or new experiences like going somewhere nice for dinner, spending time with people you love and travelling or doing something adventurous.

You can also find joy in your personal growth or discovering something new about yourself like learning a new skill or reflecting on your past accomplishments.

And finally, you can find joy in doing something meaningful like honouring your values, helping someone out or doing something that really matters to you.

These are just suggestions, explore and find what works for you but most importantly even when you don't feel like it, still find your joy. Starting might feel like an effort, but once you do, you'll see how amazing it is. For example, I have #TiwaTime carved out in my diary for my joy. You might think it's extra, but putting it in the diary helps prioritise it. Get unapologetic about doing what brings you joy. Prioritise your happiness and it will boost your positivity.

✦ GRATITUDE JOURNALING

This right here is an absolute game-changer! There's ample data to show that practising gratitude can lead to greater levels of happiness and better mental health. An article from Harvard Medical School documented a study where participants were divided into groups and asked to write a few sentences each week. One group wrote about things they were grateful for that had occurred during the week, a second group wrote about daily irritations or things that had upset them, and the third wrote about events that had affected them, with no emphasis on them being positive or negative. After ten weeks, the results showed that those who had written about gratitude were more optimistic and felt better about their lives.

Surprisingly, they also exercised more and had fewer visits to physicians than those who focused on sources of aggravation.[5] Gratitude helps you have more positive emotions, relish good experiences, improve your health, deal with adversity, and build strong relationships. Now who doesn't need that?

Here's how to do it:

○   Every evening, write down three to five things that went well for you that day. When you do this, your brain will begin to scan your day for all the positive things that have happened to you. As you begin to feel into and relive those moments, you boost your mental and emotional state and you also start seeing life is not as bad as it may seem. When you're stressed about what's missing or going wrong in your life, focusing on what's going right is a great way to start turning things around. Try to make sure you write something different every day, so it doesn't get repetitive.

○   When you write down what went well and what you're grateful for, lean into the emotion. Feel the excitement, pride, joy, confidence, sassiness, creativity, as you remember how it went. As a bonus, you could also spot any strengths you demonstrated in those moments.

○   Another way to practise gratitude is by writing a thank-you note to someone once a month. Think of someone you really want to appreciate, someone who has had a positive impact on your life. Send them a message or email expressing your gratitude for them. I really love this idea because not only do you get to practise gratitude, you also get to put a smile on someone's face and nurture your relationships.

If you've been suffering with a negative mind your whole life and haven't thought change was possible, I hope this chapter has inspired you to embrace your power and give yourself a chance. Confidence isn't the absence of self-doubt or negativity. It isn't possible to erase negative thoughts or emotions from your life completely. But it is possible to get sassy with the Mean Girl in your mind. Do it, because not every negative thing you believe about yourself is true. Getting inquisitive when self-doubt arises and replacing it with a more empowering thought is a skill you're going to need and use time and time again. You're especially going to need it in moments when you're questioning your capabilities, trying to overcome fear and putting yourself out there – as you will. Remember your emotions are just the language your body uses to speak to you. Acknowledge them, articulate them and move forward. Try not to be so obsessed with happiness that you become afraid or ashamed of less shiny emotions like pain, anxiety and fear. How you feel *is not* who you are. You are more than your depression. You are more than your anxiety and your trauma. Emotions come and go, but your worth? Baby girl, that's *here to stay!*

You are more than your anxiety and your trauma. Emotions come and go, but your worth? Baby girl, that's *here to stay!*

3

REALISING THAT YOU ARE CAPABLE

In the introduction, we defined confidence as 'the belief that you are capable of succeeding in whatever you want to do in life and become whoever you want to be'. It's a belief in your ability to succeed on your own terms. In this chapter we're going to break that down and start exploring what believing in your abilities *actually* looks and feels like.

So far you've gained a better understanding of your strengths and passions, and you've also learned some practical ways to deal with self-doubt, but as you get more curious about that inner greatness, you're bound to experience more hurdles. A part of you may be thinking, 'I see my potential, but am I *really* capable of making my dreams happen? Can I really own my own house? Can I really land my dream job? Can I really find true love and start a family? Can I really travel solo? Can I really take time off without my business crumbling?' Everything might feel so big and so overwhelming that you don't even know where to start.

I know where you're coming from. It's easier to disqualify yourself from your dreams and sit out of them than it is to take the risk, go after what you want, see if you're capable and potentially face the pain of rejection or failure if things don't work out as planned.

You may feel you just don't measure up, but the truth is:

**Knowledge and capability are
not the same thing.**

#CAKIMantra

CONFIDENT AND KILLING IT

KNOWLEDGE AND CAPABILITY ARE NOT THE SAME THING

#CAKIMantra

Just because you don't know *how* to do something doesn't mean you're not *capable* of doing it. Just because you don't know *how* to achieve a dream doesn't mean you're not *capable* of achieving that dream. Read that again. Whatever you don't know can be learned. This is where a growth mindset comes into play.

A GROWTH MINDSET

Leads to a desire to learn and a tendency to:

✦ Embrace challenges and not expect life to be perfect.

✦ Persist in the face of setbacks rather than give up.

✦ Understand the importance of habits and see hard work as the path to mastery.

✦ Learn from criticism and not assume the responsibility for pleasing everyone.

✦ Be driven by a strong sense of purpose and vision.

✦ Find lessons and inspiration in the success of others.

Some adults don't know how to drive, but that doesn't mean they aren't capable of it. If they wanted to drive, they could get the books, take the lessons, take the tests and start driving. The *capability* is within them, they just haven't invested the time and effort in breaking the challenge down and taking the steps to learn.

I once saw a tweet that said: 'Don't boo yourself off stage before you've even had the chance to perform.' What a mic-drop moment.

Right now you might have a big dream, a dream you've not even told people about because it sounds so above you that they'll think you're crazy and probably laugh at you. I want you to know you are not crazy. You are capable. So please stop disqualifying yourself from your dreams and opportunities before you've had the chance to pursue them.

Just because you don't know *how* to achieve a dream doesn't mean you're not *capable* of achieving that dream.

LEARNING AND LEVELLING UP

Society says if you don't know how to do something just 'fake it till you make it', but something about that didn't sit well with me, so I created a more empowering concept: Learning and Levelling Up.

Here's why: when you fake it till you make it, you're subconsciously saying, 'I'm a fraud and I have to be someone else to be successful.' This mindset pushes you away from your true authentic self. You're saying, 'Who I am right now isn't good enough, so I need to act as someone else [typically a man] to get ahead.' This sets a bad precedent for building confidence. First of all, it's literally asking for imposter syndrome to come into your life, and secondly, you don't need to think like a man or wear trousers to feel capable.

With Learning and Levelling Up, you acknowledge that you don't know it all or have it all and that's OK! You acknowledge your limitations, but you know that the skills and knowledge you need to succeed can be yours with hard work, practice, learning and community support.

I'm grateful that as a child I saw very good examples of Learning and Levelling Up in action. My loving and supportive dad would always say, 'What doesn't talk can't be smarter than you. Take your time, you will figure it out' – a saying he learned from his own mother. And my maternal grandma, a pioneering Scottish woman who fell in love with a charming Nigerian man at the Ashmolean Museum in Oxford, left everything she knew to start a new life in Nigeria. She arrived by ship in the Sixties not knowing anything about Nigerian people and culture, but she was determined to learn. By the end of her life, she had levelled up big time. Nothing could have prepared her for the number of challenges she would experience in her early days, but through it all she believed in her capabilities and learned as she went along. She became a fashion icon in Lagos city, dressing first ladies, hosting fashion shows, teaching women how to tie-dye local fabrics, running community projects and creating support groups for other expatriate women. She left an amazing legacy and impacted the lives of hundreds of women.

Learning and Levelling Up is an empowering perspective because it gives you ownership of your life. You dissect your dreams, see where you come in strong vs where the gaps are and then you get intentional about improving your skills while making progress towards your dreams. Your shortcomings are no longer a reason for you to sit on the sidelines or hide your true self, they are simply a guiding light indicating where you need to grow. And guess what? We all need to grow.

With this mindset, learning becomes your superpower. You stop being afraid of walking onto the stage of your life because you can always learn and practise what's needed before show time.

If you believe you're capable even when you don't have all the answers, you give yourself a chance.

You realise that you are capable, you believe you are worthy of making your dreams come true and you bet on yourself. What you believe about yourself is the foundation of everything you do and become. If you believe you're capable even when you don't have all the answers, you give yourself a chance. When you give yourself a chance, there's still a possibility you might fail, *but* there's also a possibility you might succeed, so lean into that possibility.

Newsflash: There's no shame in saying, 'I don't know.'

We're all learning as we go along. Life is so complicated, dynamic and unpredictable it's impossible to know *everything*. So be kind to yourself, because no matter how much you learn, there will always be something you don't know. This is why you can't wait until you've ticked all the boxes before you take action. You've got to learn a little, apply your knowledge, then learn some more.

Dr Valerie Young, author of *The Secret Thoughts of Successful Women: Why Capable People Suffer from the Impostor Syndrome and How to Thrive in Spite of It*, says, 'Your notion of what it means to be competent has a powerful impact on how competent you feel… Everyone experiences bouts of self-doubt from time to time – especially when attempting something new. But because "impostors" have insanely high self-expectations, the self-doubt is chronic.'

In her research, she noticed people who suffer with imposter syndrome can be grouped into five personas, based on the following type of thinking:

If I were really intelligent, capable, competent...

○   I would know everything in my field and always have an answer (The Expert).

○   I would never make a mistake or fail, it would always go according to plan (The Perfectionist).

○   I would always feel confident and excel in everything I did (The Superhuman).

○   I would get it right the first time and never struggle (The Natural Genius).

○   I would never need help (The Soloist).

With such high unsustainable and unrealistic standards, it's no surprise many of us feel like we're fakes and frauds. I've seen some really smart people with low confidence and that's because confidence is action focused, it's not about how smart you are. You can have all the knowledge in the world, but if you never bet on yourself, take action and apply your learning, you will not be confident.

> ### CONFIDENT AND KILLING IT IN ACTION
>
> *An incredibly skilled doctor came to one of my group coaching sessions and shared how she struggled with imposter syndrome whenever she had to speak at conferences, because she felt everyone was much smarter than her and she wouldn't be able to do justice to the research she was presenting. Imagine going to medical school for at least five years, training for another seven years and still feeling you're not good enough to present work you've spent over two years researching? This doctor was displaying traits of the Expert persona. She was worrying so much about the possibility of not having the answer when put to the test that she almost disqualified herself from an opportunity to grow.*
>
> *To work through it, I first got her to reflect on her strengths, as we did in Chapter 1, so she could clearly remember why she deserved to be in that room. Next, we got sassy with her Mean Girl, who was telling her she was going to flunk it, and created a more empowering narrative. Finally, we let go of the need to know it all and have all the answers and focused on creating a bounce back plan if she did get caught off-guard.*

If you want to get ahead, remember you don't need to have all the answers. Just learn a bit, do something with it, learn some more and keep evolving.

When you tap into a growth mindset and create a clear mental picture of who you want to be and the life you want to live, something magical happens. You start to notice opportunities that you didn't notice in the past, you become excited by what you can achieve, and you begin to see the steps you need to take to level up.

HOW I APPLIED LEARNING AND LEVELLING UP TO MY LIFE

In September 2019, I felt a deep pain inside me. Whenever it was time to wake up in the morning and go to work, my chest was tight, and sometimes I would struggle to breathe. I felt a deep sense of panic whenever I walked into the office. As someone who had never really struggled with anxiety, these sensations were quite new to me and I could sense the alarm bells going off.

No one did anything terrible to me, and I didn't suddenly start hating my job. In fact, I loved my job. I felt fulfilled by my work to an extent, but looking back at it, the anxiety was a signal from my higher self. It was a sign that I had outgrown my job.

My higher self had been calling me to something bigger for a while, but although I had been working on my growth mindset for about five years and knew the importance of embracing challenges and taking risks, I still ignored the nudges. That's the thing about personal growth. It's not a linear journey. Sometimes you'll know what's the right thing to do but still give in to fear. Because I was scared, I ignored the prompts until they began to manifest as anxiety in my body. My higher self was screaming, 'Baby girl, it's time to go!'

Confident and Killing It was very much still a side hustle then. I was making about £200 a month from it. I had no major clients and no speaking engagements lined up, apart from the odd university society. I didn't even know what my main business proposition was.

One Friday after a successful team meeting for one of the projects I was running, I got back to my desk, looked out of the window and a few silent tears started running down my face. I was so confused. I just had a great meeting, so why was I randomly crying? Then it dawned on me: staying in the safety of my day job when I was being pulled into starting my own movement was stifling my growth and it was hurting me. There was tension between my desire to play safe (my fixed mindset) and the growth mindset that I had been working on all these years. That tension was causing a lot of pain and, as they say, there comes a time when the pain of staying in the familiar becomes more than the fear of the unknown.

Right then and there, I got back into my growth mindset and turned down the volume of the fear by remembering the compelling vision of the impact I could make by taking my side hustle to the next level. I remembered the teenage girls I had mentored in Oxford who needed more positive and empowering messages in the media.

Leaning into my purpose gave me the fuel I needed to be brave. I grabbed my phone, walked to the bathroom, wiped my tears and called my manager to let him know I would not be returning after December. He was so kind and understanding and as soon as I dropped the phone it was as if a weight had lifted off my shoulders. I felt an immense sense of freedom and joy and immediately knew I had made the right decision.

December came. I said goodbye to my team and went off to Lagos to spend Christmas with my family, eat, sleep and step into my part time role as the minister of enjoyment.

I had no idea how I was going to make it work, but I said, 'I'll give myself three months, until March 2020, to build a sustainable business.' I had three months' worth of savings, so my plan made sense. Little did I know that 2020 had her own plans.

January actually started off really well. At the start of the New Year, I got a message from Sharmadean Reid, MBE, asking me if I could help out with a Big Woman Energy workshop she was running for her community. When she said 'help out', I envisioned handing out pens and sticky notes, until later that evening I saw *my face* on a flyer as a *speaker* at the event. I screamed, I jumped, I couldn't believe it. Before then, I had only ever spoken in classrooms to uni students. Now I would be speaking to 100 grown mission-driven women who would be there to invest in their personal growth. It was a match made in heaven.

How did I randomly get a message from the one and only Sharmadean Reid, MBE, to speak at a workshop when I had under 5,000 followers and no one established in London knew who I was or what I did?

Well, at the opening of a membership club in London, I saw her sitting with a group of friends. She's someone I always admired from afar for being a trailblazer and visionary when it came to actually empowering women, so I couldn't miss the opportunity to speak to her. I started walking in her direction then turned around. Everything in me screamed, 'Don't do it!' She was with friends, talking and having a nice time. I didn't want to be that awkward person disturbing her. I took a moment and used the Negative Thought Detector. I was making an assumption, letting fear hold me back and I would never stop a friend from seizing this opportunity. So I turned around and walked up to her.

I introduced myself and told her that I really believed in what she was doing and I was leaving my job at the end of the year, so was looking for new opportunities to align with purpose-driven women. She was super-warm and ended up emailing me a job opportunity that night to work with her company Beautystack, which is now the Stack World.

Imagine if I'd never gone up to her... Imagine if I'd let fear consume me...

You miss 100 per cent of the shots you don't take, and one thing about me, I refuse to live with regrets.

I had a look at the job description and it was a freelance role as a Beauty Scout, which involved finding new and upcoming beauty professionals, onboarding them onto the Beautystack platform and making sure they felt confident, were in a good head space and enjoyed the experience. Now I didn't really know much about the beauty industry in the UK and I didn't really want to get into it, but one thing I could do was make women feel confident! So I replied saying I didn't think the opportunity was right for me, but I would still love to have a meeting with her to pitch some other ideas.

She said, 'Cool,' and her assistant set up the meeting.

Did I actually have another idea? No. But I knew I would figure something out before the meeting. I just wanted to get my foot in the door somehow, because I knew she would love me.

Remember:

Knowledge and capability are not the same thing.

#CAKIMantra

Just because I didn't know what to do didn't mean I wasn't capable of making it work. I was determined to make it work, and as soon as I gave my mind a *clear* goal I began thinking outside the box. Here's some insight into my thought process:

How could I help beauty pros feel more confident? Hmmm... Well, mindset always comes first, so they'll need to think *like a pro... Once their mind is programmed for success, they'll need to communicate their value, so..*

Talk like a pro...

and then they'll put it all together, show up and act *like a pro...*

Boom! My idea for the Beauty Pro School was born.

I used Canva, a graphic design platform to create a snazzy deck of three bespoke workshops, 'Think like a Pro', 'Talk like a Pro' and 'Act like a Pro', designed for the beauty pros that someone else would scout and I would offer confidence coaching services as an add-on for the pros after the three workshops. I was Learning and Levelling Up.

I really want to emphasise this idea came to me *after* I arranged a meeting to pitch the idea. Having a growth mindset pushes you to take risks (that often pay off in the end), because you understand that knowledge can be acquired and intelligence can be developed, and even if it doesn't work out, failure isn't a sign of lack of intelligence but an opportunity to learn more and make better decisions next time. Even when you don't have all the answers, it's important that you give yourself the chance to make your dreams happen. If I hadn't walked up to Sharmadean that night, I would have blocked my blessings.

Even if it doesn't work out, failure isn't a sign of lack of intelligence but an opportunity to learn more and make better decisions next time.

Sis, pleaseee don't block your blessings. Not everything in life is going to happen the way you want, but you should never be the one to sabotage your own self. There's enough bad vibes in the world as it is, so never be the one to block *your own* blessings.

As you can imagine, Sharmadean loved the idea and gave the green light for it to go ahead in March 2020. I was now on her radar, which is why she got in touch about the Big Woman Energy workshop in January 2020. Mission accomplished.

That session in January was a massive success and I started getting more visibility through word of mouth. I would also go to a bunch of events, find the organisers at the end and pitch myself to them as a speaker for their next event. It was working. My bank account still looked pretty miserable, but the next three months were looking promising and I had high hopes for International Women's Day that year.

Then lockdown happened and E.V.E.R.Y.T.H.I.N.G. got cancelled. *Everything.* Cancellation email after cancellation email after cancellation email. Gosh, I cried some ugly tears. You know, the tears when you're just curled up in bed, hugging a bowl of popcorn and drinking wine, or crying those sad Nineties music video shower tears. Yup, I was down bad! No one wanted to try Zoom, everyone was panicking, everyone was stressed, people were losing jobs, and the last thing they wanted to think about was a personal development workshop.

My Mean Girl was having a blast, of course. She told me it was over, it was time to look for other jobs, because, let's be honest, there was no way out of this. An image of myself going up and then crashing down played over and over in my head. It looked like the graph below. A complete dead end.

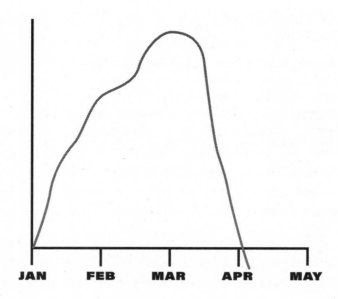

JAN   FEB   MAR   APR   MAY

After a few weeks of tears and sitting with my emotions, I had been through two of the 3As for processing negative emotions. I had acknowledged my feelings, I had articulated what was going on, and now it was time to allow myself to move forward. I looked at myself in the mirror and my growth mindset prompted me to reframe my situation.

'Tiwa, is this the story you want for yourself? That the pandemic happened, you lost all your business and gave up?'

'No – that's not, it's not the story I want.'

'OK then, what story *do you* want?'

I wrote:

o I want to see more growth in my business than I've ever seen before.

o I want to build a global community of women.

o I really, really, really want to equip women with the tools and mindset they need to take action and win in life.

o I want 'Confident and Killing It' to be a household name.

And as I wrote those words, my heart gave me a resounding 'Yes!' I could feel it in my gut. When you connect with your truth, your heart will always tell you you're on the right path.

That was the last time I felt sorry for myself. So I redrew the graph with the vision of how I knew things could play out if I allowed my capabilities the space to thrive and focused on the positive vision of my hopes and desires instead of the negativity my mind was pushing on me. It looked something like this:

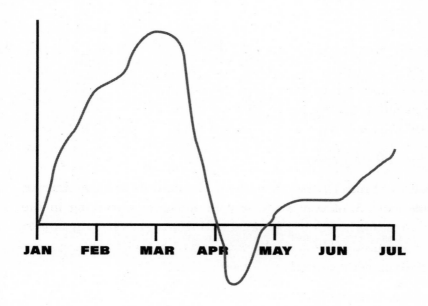

At the top I wrote: 'Whatever goes down must come back up. I am #unstoppable.'

It was in that moment that I remembered that 'unstoppable' was my favourite word to describe myself, and not because I felt life would be a breeze and I would never get hit. It was my word because whenever I *did* get hit, I always, always, bounced back. Before the pandemic I had never given up on myself and I definitely wasn't going to start now.

This was me in March 2020: less than £1,000 in my bank account, no bookings, no work, *but* a vision – a vision powerful enough to carry me through the storm and unlock a level of growth I hadn't even imagined yet.

The key lessons from my story? Invest in your mindset, define your dream, believe you are capable of making it a reality and grow through your challenges. Energy flows where attention goes. It's good to know what you don't want in life, but even more important to know what you *do* want! That's where a lot of us fall down. We know what we're bad at. We know what we hate. We know what we're afraid of. We know how we don't want life to go, but do we spend any time visualising the future we *actually* want for ourselves? Do you look at situations from a growth mindset perspective, as we learned in the last chapter, and see how it can work in your favour? Everything in the physical world was first created in the mind. So if all the energy in your mind is being used to focus on what you *don't* like, guess what you get more of?

Take a moment, park the fear and doubt to one side and just dream! Don't worry about how to make that dream happen just yet, just dream. In *Psycho-Cybernetics*, a self-help book written in 1960, after an extensive study on self-image and the mind, author Maxwell Maltz concluded that:

> *'All your actions, feelings, behaviours, even your abilities, are always consistent with your self-image. You will act like the sort of person you conceive yourself to be. If you conceive yourself as a failure-type person, you will find a way to fail.'*

And I'll add if you conceive yourself as a successful and capable-type person, you will find a way to succeed. Don't worry too much about how exactly it will happen, just start with the resources available to you and be ready for when opportunities strike. Once you believe an answer to your problem or challenge already exists, everything within you conspires to uncover the solution.

Just to be clear, my definition of success isn't just about becoming financially wealthy. In Chapter 7 I unpack how to come up with your own definition of 'Killing It' and succeed on your own terms, but my focus in this chapter is on helping you see that you are capable of creating a fulfilling life. I know there are a lot of socio-economic factors that affect a person's ability to achieve and succeed, and given all we've been through as a collective during the COVID-19 pandemic, I want to acknowledge that some of us might be experiencing challenges that we can't just positively think our way out of. Deep-rooted structural issues like a lack of affordable childcare and housing aren't the responsibility of the individual. We may not all have the same resources and opportunities, but we can all believe we are worthy and capable of living a full life. Regardless of your background or status, you deserve to have some dreams, and whether they're big or small, you deserve to know that you are worthy of seeing them become a reality.

Once I had supplied my mind with the vision, it started to give me ideas on how to make it happen. I had never run a business before, not to mention in a pandemic, but I knew learning was my superpower, and it's yours too. One of the things I remembered learning in my previous job as a partnerships manager was the power of collaborations when growing your brand. So I used my transferable skills, did some research on how to write pitch emails and reached out to some incredible female entrepreneurs to ask if they would like to join me in the free online webinar series I was going to start running, called 'Killing It as an Entrepreneur'.

Looking back, the irony of that name makes me laugh. At the time I was far from killing it as an entrepreneur. I had no idea what I was doing, but I didn't focus on the things I didn't know, I relied on my existing knowledge, my transferable skills, my self-belief, my ability to Learn and Level Up, my faith and the support from my family and community.

Some of you might be thinking, 'Yeah, but isn't this faking it?' No, not at all. I owned where I was on my journey. I was also learning in those sessions. I didn't show up acting like I knew it all and was a successful entrepreneur, I showed up with a growth mindset. I thought, 'I'm just starting this journey, I want to kill it and I know there are women out there who also want to kill it, so let's come together and figure it out.'

It was meant to be one single event, but after 500 women signed up, I knew I had unlocked something major. I'm trying really hard not to cry as I write this, because looking at how far I've come on my entrepreneurial journey leaves me in awe. One webinar turned into a series of five, which saw over 1,500 women join from all over the world. I had people waking up at crazy hours in Australia and the Philippines to join sessions. My vision was unfolding.

Every other Sunday for three months I showed up consistently and that consistency began to open doors. Women who attended my webinars started inviting me to speak at organisations they worked at; I designed £20 small group masterclasses for anyone who wanted to dive deeper after the webinar and promoted it during the webinar and on Instagram so I could start making some income. I finished my life-coaching qualification, increased my prices and also launched a podcast to demonstrate my expertise as a confidence coach, so if people were curious or sceptical about my work, they could listen for free before booking me. By

December 2020 I had run workshops for employees at Google, Deloitte, Morgan Stanley, TikTok, Depop, Meta (Facebook), YouTube and Snapchat, coached over fifty women across four countries and recorded 16,000 downloads on the podcast.

Ding, ding, ding! Tiwa 1 – 0 Pandemic

Did I know this was all going to happen back in March? Did I even know *how* it was going to happen? No. Remember I spent my days crying and eating popcorn and cookies from Sainsburys, because I thought it was all over.

Just because you don't know the way through your challenges doesn't mean you aren't capable of overcoming them.

#CAKIMantra

JUST BECAUSE YOU DON'T KNOW THE WAY THROUGH YOUR CHALLENGES DOESN'T MEAN YOU AREN'T CAPABLE OF OVERCOMING THEM.

#CAKIMantra

Read that again.

I learned from the women who had gone before me, I practised behind the scenes, I created my own opportunities and I Levelled Up.

I'm sharing this story because I want you to know if I can do it, you can do it too. I'm not special, I'm an everyday woman who has learned to master her mind and believe there is a greatness within her – a greatness that is within you too. You just have to wake up to it.

If you feel a bit jealous or salty as you read this, stop everything you're doing and jump to Chapter 8: Embracing Your Main Character Energy.

If you feel inspired and motivated to create a compelling vision for your life and achieve it, keep reading.

Here's a quick recap:

HOW IT STARTED	HOW IT'S GOING
March 2020 Vision	**December 2021 Progress**
I want to see more growth in my business than I've ever seen before.	I now run a six-figure business.
I want to build a global community of women.	The *Confident and Killing It* podcast is listened to in 153 different countries and women in over fifty countries attend my webinars.
I really, really, really want to equip women with the tools and mindset they need to take action and win in life.	I launched my course 'The Confidence Game Plan', a five-step action plan to becoming confident, and an academy so women could get courses, coaching and community support all in one place. Wrote a book! Podcast is growing and is now on 60,000 downloads. One workshop with Google has led to four and my list of corporate clients is growing.
I want 'Confident and Killing It' to be a household name.	This is still a work in progress, but trust me, after this book, it's going to happen and Oprah is going to interview me one day.

When you tap into a growth mindset and believe you are capable, you will be *unstoppable.*

The evidence is clear: something magical happens when you have a growth mindset and a clear vision of what you want. Even when you don't know how it's going to happen, when you tap into a growth mindset and believe you are capable, you will be *unstoppable*.

CONFIDENT AND KILLING IT IN ACTION

I'm no rare coincidence. One of my clients, Sarah, founder of Farm Girl Goes Vegan, is another example of the greatness you can unlock when you combine a growth mindset with a clear vision. Her vision was to make going vegan look fun and easy by building a judgement-free community and a purpose-driven business that helps the environment. However, when she came to me for coaching, she had a fixed mindset with a lot of self-doubt and mental roadblocks. Using all the tools and techniques in this book, I helped her cultivate a growth mindset and just look at how she levelled up:

HOW IT STARTED

Fixed mindset with a vision

Worked in a corporate job that she didn't really like for eight years, was trapped in a mindset of 'I just need to pay my bills.'

Had a vision but put it on the back burner.

Was too scared of leaving her full-time job to build her vegan business because she didn't have the belief that she could succeed at anything except working for someone else.

HOW IT'S GOING

Growth mindset with a vision

Made the decision to prioritise her confidence and growth and never looked back. Gave herself five months to quit her full-time job and become a full-time entrepreneur, which she did!

Had her wake-up moment in our Power Circle session where she realised she had all the strengths, skills and passion to succeed as a vegan entrepreneur.

Started being more intentional about building her online community and showing up more consistently.

Launched a course on easy steps to go vegan.

Started pitching to brands to get paid for content creation and confidently negotiated higher rates.

Started positioning herself as a thought leader and got invited to speak on podcasts and at corporate events.

Feeling extremely unhappy and on the verge of really poor mental health because of the high levels of unfulfilment.

Thinking of her vision whilst feeling helpless and stuck was disheartening.

Is the happiest she's ever been in a long time. In our catch-up call she said:

'I feel like I'm exactly where I'm supposed to be. I'm aligned with my vision and I get to live a life that *I chose.* My confidence and growth mindset have been my anchor on days when I felt like giving up. Knowing where I want to go and having confidence in my ability to get there really is a magical combination.'

If both Sarah and I can do it, you totally can too. If you've got a big vision but don't feel capable enough to go after it the next tool will help with that. Let's get into it.

LEVEL-UP:

SEVEN STEPS TO REALISING YOUR CAPABILITY

You're not going to attempt to take action on a dream if you don't think you're qualified in the first place, so here are seven questions you can ask yourself to help you get more comfortable going after big, audacious and scary dreams:

1. **'What's the dream/goal that feels a bit scary?'** Always start by defining and writing out what the dream is. Don't just leave it as a thought in your head. _____

    _____

    _____

2. **'Is this dream in line with my Power Circle?'** If so, carry on to the next step; if not, then revisit your Power Circle and tweak the dream. _____

    _____

    _____

    _____

3. **'Why is this dream or goal important to me?'** Having an emotional connection with your dreams helps you feel more inspired and motivated to take action. _____

_____

_____

4. **'What internal resources do I have to potentially make this work?'** Reflect on your strengths, passions, values and skills. _____

_____

_____

5. **'What external resources do I have that I can make use of now and in the future?'** Reflect on your professional network, community, technology, government schemes etc.

_____

_____

_____

6. **'What three things can I start doing today/this week to get one baby step closer to my dream?'** Don't worry if this feels scary, we'll tackle the fear later on; just write it down. _____

_____

_____

7. **'What areas do I need to Learn and Level Up in to increase my chances of success with this dream?'** Once you've identified the knowledge or skill gaps between where you are and where you want to be, set goals to start working on them. For example, completing a marketing course or learning another language so you can live abroad. _____

_____

_____

If your knowledge gaps feel overwhelming, remember a lack of knowledge isn't a lack of capability. It's the small, consistent steps that often lead to big fundamental life changes. For example, if you want to become more financially literate and start investing, you can start by reading one article a day or listening to podcasts to learn key terms and concepts. Then you can join online financial literacy-focused communities like Female Invest, Money Medics and Juno to widen your knowledge and connect with like-minded people.

A lack of knowledge isn't a lack of capability.

Set yourself the target of improving one skill or increasing your knowledge in one area and then just focus on winning each day. We tend to overestimate what we can do in one year and underestimate what we can do in three years. One hour a day working on your personal growth is better than ten hours never. Slow and steady is better than fast and never.

Finally, it's important to work towards a big vision while staying happy and grateful in the present. Our brain is more likely to achieve success when we are happy and feeling good about ourselves. So enjoy the ride and don't despise the days of small beginnings.

DITCHING THE WEIGHT OF PERFECTIONISM AND PROCRAS-TINATION

The next few chapters are about to be bumpy. Up until this point, I've been equipping you with a new growth mindset and waking you up to your worth, strengths and capabilities. But now it's time to face some major confidence killers. Because we can't talk about building confidence without diving into some of the things that might trip you up and keep you stagnant on your journey to confidence.

When we're young, we're taught to be high-achievers and show up as our very best. This is healthy, as ambition fuels growth. But somewhere down the line in our adulting journey, we often turn into over-achievers and the unhealthy traits of perfectionism take over our life and kill our confidence. We tend to pursue perfectionism under the disguise of healthy striving or pursuing excellence, but in reality…

> **Perfectionism is just a coping mechanism to avoid criticism, blame and shame. It keeps us stuck in fear instead of moving our life forward.**
>
> **#CAKIMantra**

I've already highlighted how damaging marketing messages have been to women's and teenage girls' confidence levels over the years, so I won't go into that again. This time I'm focusing on you. Yes, you, because although you may have grown up in a perfectionist-praising over-achieving culture, you don't have to *stay* in it. You can choose to burst the bubble. You can choose

PERFECTIONISM IS JUST A

CONFIDENT AND KILLING IT

COPING MECHANISM TO AVOID CRITICISM, BLAME AND SHAME.

IT KEEPS US STUCK IN FEAR INSTEAD OF MOVING OUR LIFE FORWARD.

#CAKIMantra

to say, 'Tiwalola, I'm done with this BS, I want to live life on my own terms, with my own rules, and choose excellence over perfectionism.' So, if that's you right now, strap in, because you're going in for the best ride of your life.

Perfectionism is defined as 'a tendency to set excessively high and unrealistic standards for yourself and/or others.' Like any personality trait, it includes a whole spectrum of characteristics, some positive and some negative, that vary from person to person. Let's look at five differences between being a high-achiever (pursuing a healthy standard of excellence) and being an over-achiever (pursuing perfection). If you see yourself in any of the negative descriptions, don't freak out. I'm right here with you on this ride, there is a way out and we're going to look at some healthy alternatives together. And even if none of these descriptions are you, the culture of perfectionism that we live in is so strong, you're likely to spot these traits in some of your friends, colleagues and loved ones. When you do, use the insights from this book to spark a conversation and nudge them from living under the weight of perfectionism to enjoying the freedom of self-love and confidence. Life is more fun when we're *all* free from perfectionism and shame.

PERFECTIONISM: THE HEALTHY AND UNHEALTHY TRAITS

So, are you a *high*-achiever or are you an *over*-achiever? Let's get into it!

When it comes to setting goals and targets...

○ Over-achievers will often set their initial goals out of reach, with crazy deadlines that move them past the 'stretch zone' into the 'stress zone'.[1] It's one thing to go the extra mile, but it's another thing to overstretch yourself and burn out, which is what pursuing goals often feels like for over-achievers.

○ High-achievers also set high goals, but these goals are within reach, with deadlines that are realistic. They stretch themselves and are ambitious, but know their boundaries and won't sacrifice their health in order to achieve their goals.

When it comes to achieving their goals...

○ Over-achievers will prioritise outcomes over people, health, relationships and personal joy. They are laser-focused on the end result, and the way in which they go after the goal often outweighs the reward. They are ready to take down anything or anyone that gets in their way and often feel frustrated when the goal takes a while to achieve.

○ High-achievers focus more on the journey than the goal. They see the beauty in the process and understand that's where the real lessons of wisdom lie. They stay mindful and find fulfilment in the present moment while working towards their final destination.

For example, let's say you start a new sport or hobby like boxing or sewing. You don't become a pro overnight and have to spend hours learning techniques, practising one move before moving to the next. If you are an over-achiever, you may compare yourself to someone who's been doing it for five years or more and wonder when you'll finally be good enough, and every day will feel like a drain. If you adopt the mindset of a high-achiever, however, you'll focus on the present moment and celebrate each new skill or level you unlock, and every day you'll be more motivated as you improve.

When it comes to measuring their progress and defining success...

○ Over-achievers will accept nothing less than perfect. Any result that isn't an accomplishment of the original overly ambitious goal is seen as a failure. No buts – if they haven't ticked all the boxes, then they've failed. They've either done it all or achieved absolutely nothing. Life is often seen as black or white, either/or.

○ High-achievers, on the other hand, will experience some level of satisfaction and pride for doing a great job even if they didn't completely reach their original target. Rather than obsess over results, they see success as any step in the right direction and acknowledge that slow progress is *still* progress and worthy of celebration.

When it comes to reviewing their personal performance...

○   Over-achievers find it easier to spot their mistakes and tend to amplify their imperfections. They focus on all the things that went wrong and fail to spot the silver lining. They also internalise failure as something being wrong with them, wallow in negativity and are highly critical of themselves, which tends to lead to depression and anxiety. If they do happen to do something well, rather than feeling pride or joy in their accomplishments, they are simply relieved that they have not failed.

○   High-achievers take pride in their accomplishments and celebrate their wins. They don't compare their performance to that of other people, so tend to be more supportive of others' successes than over-achievers. When things go wrong, they don't let failure define them. Instead, they maintain a strong sense of self-worth, treat themselves with compassion, reframe failure as a stepping stone to success and bounce back stronger than ever.

When it comes to receiving constructive criticism from others...

o   Because a less-than-perfect performance is so painful and scary to over-achievers, they tend to take constructive criticism badly and see it as a personal attack. They get defensive, shut down and dismiss any suggestions to help them grow.

o   High-achievers, on the other hand, see constructive criticism as really valuable information and use it as motivation to grow, learn and level up. They don't feel that anybody is 'out to get them' and instead appreciate the openness and honesty of the feedback. They realise they aren't defined by their limitations and embrace life as a journey of growth and development.

If we recap on the traits of over-achievers and what they experience as a result of this behaviour and thinking, you will see that this is really, really, really *not* the direction you want your life to go in:

They set unrealistic expectations.	○ Stress
	○ Anxiety
They only focus on the outcome and will sacrifice health, happiness and relationships to achieve their goals.	○ Depression and other mental health issues
	○ Self-sabotage
	○ Fear
They are obsessed with ticking ALL of the boxes and anything short of the original target is 100 per cent failure.	○ Burnout
	○ Physical body pains
	○ Lack of motivation
They spot mistakes and dwell on them continuously.	○ Low confidence
	○ Procrastination
They internalise failure and criticism as them not being good enough.	○ Unfulfilment
	○ Isolation
	○ Insomia

In the short term, you might feel that being a perfectionist is working for you. It can lead to some progress and success, *but* in the long term it's not sustainable at all. Setting unrealistic targets for yourself over and over again will lead to severe burnout, stress and anxiety. It's also very likely that when you think perfectionism is working for you, it's because you're tapping into the traits of a high-achiever rather than an over-achiever. So if you'd like to stress less and achieve more, ditching perfectionism is the best thing you can do for yourself.

CHOOSING VULNERABILITY

Brené Brown, *New York Times* bestselling author and researcher pioneering the vulnerability discourse, describes perfectionism as:

> *...the ultimate fear that the world is going to see us for who we really are and we won't measure up. As a result we end up walking around with a 20-ton shield, hoping it will protect us, but it actually stops us from being seen. Vulnerability on the other hand is the willingness to show up and be seen with no guarantee of the outcome. People often see vulnerability as a weakness, but vulnerability sounds like truth and courage. Truth and courage aren't always comfortable, but they are never a weakness.[2]*

Admitting you aren't perfect, admitting you've failed, admitting that you are sometimes afraid takes a whole lot of courage and strength, but the beauty of vulnerability is that you can be all those things *and* still see yourself as someone who is worthy of love and belonging, someone who is brave, strong and excellent. Vulnerability isn't either/or, it embraces the multi-dimensional nature of being human. It allows you to see the beauty in your strengths *and* your struggles, instead of obsessing over your strengths and hiding your weaknesses, as perfectionists do.

Clare Seal, the author of *Real Life Money* and mastermind behind @myfrugalyear on Instagram, documented her struggles as she and her family went through a period of trying to get free of £27k debt. As she shared some of her mistakes with her community on social media, she also celebrated small victories and shared new lessons to make sure others could learn from her. She embraced her money struggles while also embracing her newfound discipline, creativity and emotional intelligence.

Another example is Stephanie Yeboah, author of *Fattily Ever After*, who I interviewed in episode 28 of the *Confident and Killing It* podcast. She shares her struggles living at the intersection of a fatphobic, misogynistic and racist society that projects inadequacy onto her as a fat Black woman, but also shows beautiful moments of strength as she shows up in full force (regardless of the haters), loving every part of her and being totally unapologetic about being – as she says – 'a fat girl with opinions'.

When you embrace and speak up about what the world expects you to be ashamed of, shame cannot thrive.

The confidence lesson from how these two women use vulnerability as a superpower is that when you embrace and speak up about what the world expects you to be ashamed of, shame cannot thrive. It loses its power and you gain yours.

In her book *Daring Greatly* Brené Brown says, 'There's a crack in everything, that's how the light gets in,' so don't be afraid of your cracks and imperfections, because they present the perfect opportunity for growth.

In life, most people want to be seen, want to be heard, want to know that they matter, and ultimately want to know that there is meaning and purpose in their lives. Perfectionism takes us away from that and vulnerability takes us towards that. Perfectionism keeps us standing on the sidelines of our life, hiding at the back, on our tiptoes, looking in and wondering what it would be like if we had the courage to show up just as we are. This is a dangerous, limiting and hurtful place to be.

Vulnerability, on the other hand, allows us to show up with confidence and step into our life because who we are right now is good enough. It takes us towards our purpose and gives us a true sense of freedom, so we can go out into our world with confidence and kill it on our own terms.

PRACTICAL VULNERABILITY

Now that we've looked at the power of vulnerability, let's look at how to get practical with it. Authenticity and vulnerability are a practice. We have to make the choice every day to let our authentic selves be seen by others and embrace all of who we are in order to live more fully.

Start from within

Here are some questions to get you opening up so you can have a deep conversation with yourself:

1. 'Why do I feel the need to be perfect?'

2. 'Who do I want to be perfect for?'

3. 'Where will being perfect lead me?' (Hint: Remember the diagram on page 155.)

4. 'What parts of my life am I looking to be perfect in to conceal or hide what is currently there?'

5. 'What am I afraid will happen if I'm not perfect?'

6. 'Is the way I'm thinking and acting in alignment with my core values?'

7. 'How do I hold space for my emotions and feelings?'

8. 'What's worth doing even if I fail?'

9. 'What does vulnerability look like and mean to me?'

10. 'Who do I feel comfortable sharing with?'

Take risks and start before you're ready

Be willing to throw yourself in, take risks and bet on yourself. Get adventurous and do things outside your comfort zone that you've never done before so you can practise failing and getting back up again. The pain of regret is worse than the pain of trying and failing. The people you're playing it safe for are busy living their own lives; isn't it time you live yours?

Examples:

✦ Asking to be paid more money.

✦ Saying 'I love you' first.

✦ Sharing an idea or dream with someone.

✦ Starting a new hobby.

✦ Going on a solo date or holiday.

✦ Applying for a new job even when you don't tick all the boxes.

✦ Going to a dance or drama class.

✦ Breaking the rules once in a while.

Feel free to make a list of your own and commit to doing one activity every month.

Ask for help

To a lot of people, asking for help is a weakness. In a world where we have to look as though we have it all together, asking for help is often taken as a sign that we're not skilled enough, knowledgeable enough or strong enough. But what if asking for help means we're a collaborative person? What if it means we're working smarter, because two heads are better than one? Remember, you can be strong *and* still ask for help. It's not all or nothing.

Get real with yourself for a second and think of an area in your life you could do with some help in. Don't worry about being a burden, just ask and see what happens.

I used to be one of those 'It's quicker to do it myself' people, and let me tell you that hiring an executive assistant and building a team was the best decision I've ever made, because delegation will set you free! Some things are actually quicker when you collaborate and delegate. Divide and conquer is how I roll now.

Openly embrace your struggles

Remember I said there was beauty in your strengths and your struggles? Well, actively acknowledging and sharing your struggles is a good way to practise vulnerability. On my Instagram page I have a highlight called 'Struggles', because I never want anyone to come on my page and go, 'She's so perfect, she's confident all the time.' That's not true. I have my fair share of struggles, and as someone who is in the public eye a lot, sharing my struggles actually helps me build a deeper connection with my community. So just as it's important to share your wins, it's important to be transparent and share the lessons you've learned from your mistakes, failures and dark seasons.

A word of caution though: vulnerability isn't about sharing with everyone all the time. You've got to set boundaries with it. Share when you feel safe, know what/when to share with people close to you and know what/when to share with your wider community. This is very subjective, but I prefer to share when I feel I'm in a healthier head space and have processed my emotions so I'm sharing with clarity and intention. I no longer feel that my story owns me; instead, I own the story. I share when I can see the light at the end of the tunnel and not when I'm right in the middle of the storm.

If you feel a bit of regret after you've been publicly vulnerable, that's all part of it. Let the emotion come and go and know that the focus is less on what you shared and more on the fact that you are worthy of being seen and heard by others in a way that feels true and authentic to you.

Be kind to yourself

Being kind to yourself is a form of vulnerability. Being open to loving yourself unconditionally, regardless of what you look like, regardless of how messy your mind is and the mistakes you've made, is vulnerability. Being kind enough to forgive yourself for poor decisions you've made in the past and give yourself another chance is vulnerability.

In my early twenties, after spending years super conscious of what I looked like because of my acne, as I mentioned earlier, I started to look into my eyes in the mirror and say, 'Tiwa, I love you.' It's an empowering practice.

TO PRACTISE SELF-COMPASSION YOU COULD ALSO:

- Prioritise your self-care.

- Write a love letter to yourself or to a specific insecurity.

- Look into the mirror regularly and read out your 'I am...' strength affirmations (see p.42).

- Set boundaries.

- Reset yourself by completing these sentences:
  '[Your name], I love you for...'
  '[Your name], I forgive you for...'
  '[Your name], I'm proud of you for...'

- Write a list of all the things you forgive yourself for, turn the page and start a new chapter.

A couple of years ago I held an event where I got women to come up and read letters they wrote to themselves about embracing their insecurities. One letter that I was completely moved by was from Toyosi Alexis who was 17 at the time.

To My Hearing Loss:

When I was younger, I didn't mind you. I don't think I was fully aware of what was going on. I just knew I had to wear these things in my ears to help me hear and attend speech therapy lessons, but I never really thought of myself as different from those around me.

But, as I got older and became more aware of the interaction and of course, judgment, I became more conscious of your presence. I became more sensitive to the looks I received from those around me when my hair was in a bun or when I asked someone to repeat themselves multiple times.

Would I be looked at with pity?

Would I be employable if I declared myself as having a 'disability'?

These questions among many more quickly became a part of my everyday life, and from this point on, I started to resent you.

Couldn't you just fix yourself and go away?

I fought to prove that I was worthy, more than just a girl with hearing aids and a weird accent. I'm now realising that I was doing all of that more for myself than for anyone around me, and honestly, I'm realising what a gift you are.

Perspective, opportunity, strength, a story – some of the many things you've given me. I'm thankful for the lessons on patience and empathy – all of which have shaped me today. All of this and so much more, I owe to you.

Thank you for being my gift, my uniqueness, my teacher, my shield of armour.

Thank you for being patient with me as I have come to these realisations.

Here's to a journey of endless teachings, genuine self-acceptance and to the woman I am to be. People around me have taught me there's beauty in being different, and I'm sorry it's taken me so long to accept you for you.

How beautiful is that? There is so much freedom available to you when you practise self-compassion and make a decision to treat yourself with the honesty, kindness and encouragement you so readily give others. By showing up fully and embracing your imperfections, people's negative words cannot have power over you.

NURTURING BODY CONFIDENCE

We can't talk about ditching the weight of perfectionism without addressing the ridiculous amount of pressure women and girls feel to have the 'perfect' body. In a world that thrives off our insecurities, being unapologetic about our body is the greatest revolution of all... while also being the greatest challenge for many of us. For years, popular culture has bombarded us with messages about how we are flawed and presented perfection as just one purchase away. I think we can all agree that the unrealistic body standards that are pervasive in all parts of society have caused a lot of damage to our self-esteem. We know bodily perfection doesn't exist, but when we look in the mirror, we can't help but pick ourselves apart. How do we begin to fix this?

✦ BODY POSITIVITY

The body positivity movement was born out of a need to reject perfectionism and promotes the acceptance of all bodies, shapes and sizes. The focus is on loving our body just the way it is and challenging negative idealistic body standards. Body positivity encourages us to prioritise loving and caring for our body and seeing the beauty in our cellulite, stretch marks and all the different parts of us that society tends to reject.

Seeing the beauty in our imperfections helps us take power back into our own hands and stops us from falling victim to society's perfectionism agenda, which, as we've seen from the diagram on page 155, can cause stress, eating disorders, poor mental health and much more. Embracing our body just as it is helps us build good self-esteem and reminds us that we are worthy of loving our body.

However, what happens when we're not in the mood to or we're really struggling to see any beauty in ourselves whatsoever? After being subconsciously told we have flaws for the majority of our life, how do we randomly wake up and just start loving ourselves? Isn't it unhealthy to force ourselves to find love that isn't there?

Bring in body neutrality.

✦ BODY NEUTRALITY

This movement suggests we take our physical appearance out of the equation completely and instead of trying to love our body no matter what, focus more on what it can do for us. Rather than loving the way our legs look, for example, we can be grateful that we have legs that allow us to move around. Rather than hating how our voice sounds, we can be grateful for our ability to speak up and use our voice in a positive way.

I also believe our bodies are *a part* of who we are, not *all* of who we are. So with body neutrality, instead of linking our physical appearance to our self-worth, we can show gratitude and appreciation for our body's unique abilities and functions.

✦ BODY CONFIDENCE

Nurturing body confidence encapsulates both mindsets, because we can love our body for how it looks, regardless of its shape or size, while also appreciating the amazing things it can do.

Just as building confidence is a bit of a rollercoaster, learning to love our body and ditch the weight of perfectionism is a similar journey. We might love our body one day and struggle to love it the next. In fact, we may never grow to love the parts of our body we're insecure about. It doesn't mean we're a failure or bad person.

For me, seeing my body as a vessel to live out my purpose actually helped me love it more, but will I ever fully and wholly love every single aspect of my body, including my 'thunder thighs'? I'm not sure and that feels like way too much pressure. Instead I'm choosing to see my body as my friend instead of my enemy. I'm choosing to be kind to my body the way I am kind to those around me. I'm choosing to give my body some grace by not having unrealistic expectations of it and know that it will disappoint me some days but it will also be there for me beyond my wildest dreams. I'm choosing to listen to what my body needs, nurture it without judgement or shame and move it in a way that makes it happy.

So, the next time a lack of confidence in your appearance prevents you from doing something you want to do, just remember that there is more to you than what you look like.

DITCHING THE WEIGHT OF PROCRASTINATION

Perfectionism and procrastination tend to go hand in hand. This is because, fearing failure as they do, perfectionists will sometimes worry so much about doing something imperfectly that they become immobilised and fail to do anything at all.

Focusing on avoiding failure doesn't lead to success. It leads to procrastination.

Let's take a quick look into your mind to understand how your thoughts affect your actions.

LEVEL-UP:

THE MINDSET BEHIND PROCRASTINATION

Motivation

○ Think of a task or activity you are usually motivated to do. You don't have to think twice about it, you love doing it and will rarely skip it. _____

_____

_____

_____

_____

○ What thoughts come to mind when you think about doing that activity? _____

_____

_____

_____

_____

○ What feelings and emotions arise when it's time to do that activity? _____

_____

_____

_____

_____

_____

Procrastination

○ Think of a task or activity you are currently procrastinating on. You keep pushing it away and deprioritising it. _____

_____

_____

_____

_____

_____

○ What thoughts come to mind when you think of doing that activity? _____

_____

_____

_____

_____

_____

○ What feelings and emotions arise when it's time to do that activity? _____

_____

_____

_____

Analysis

○ Do you notice any differences between your thoughts and emotions when you're motivated and your thoughts and emotions when you're procrastinating? _____

_____

_____

_____

_____

_____

○ What have you observed? _____

_____

_____

_____

_____

_____

Most people notice that their thoughts and emotions are positive when they are motivated and negative when they are procrastinating. This happens because:

Negative thoughts = Negative emotions = Retreating, aka procrastination

Positive thoughts = Positive emotions = Moving forward, aka motivation

It's scientifically proven that our thoughts, emotions and actions are all connected. That's why we covered mindset so early on in this book. The stories we tell ourselves are so important. We literally become what we believe ourselves to be.

So let's say you've been putting off having a difficult conversation with a friend. Your thoughts probably sound like:

'What if she takes it really badly?'

'What if it backfires on me and I'm seen as the bad person?'

'Urgh, I don't even know what to say.'

'I'm really bad at confronting people. I'm probably going to mess this up.'

'Why are friendships sooo haaaaard?'

'What if all our other friends take her side?'

All those negative thoughts are going to make you feel more worried, more anxious, more stressed and less confident. When you feel this way, you'll have absolutely no desire to confront this friend and have the difficult conversation, so you'll procrastinate and say it's not the right time.

Let's look at another example. You have a deadline coming up at work for a pitch deck you need to submit. If you're procrastinating, you're probably thinking:

'I'm not creative enough to do this. They'll probably hate my ideas.'

'Do people even care about what I have to say?'

'I hate speaking in public. I always mess up my explanations.'

'Why did they even give me this project? I'm not the best person for this job.'

'What if the client doesn't like my ideas and I get fired...? OMG!'

'I haven't done enough research. I'm not ready to start yet.'

All those thoughts will make you dread working on the pitch deck and you'll just keep pushing it back because the negativity is so overwhelming.

On the other hand, when you think positively about yourself, you tend to believe in yourself more and see your capabilities. When you see your capabilities, you're more likely to take action. When you take action, you build your confidence, make progress and get inspired to keep going.

Here are some positive ways of thinking that will encourage you to take action:

'I enjoy coming up with new concepts and thinking outside the box. What if people really like my ideas?'

'I know my voice is important and it matters. I owe it to myself to speak up.'

'Speaking in public is scary, but my message is more important than my fear. If I make a mistake, it's OK. I'm human and I'll learn from it next time.'

✦ 'I'm not always going to tick all the boxes. No one is perfect, but I am definitely capable of learning and trying new things.'

✦ 'What if the client loves my ideas? And my performance on this project lands me a promotion?'

✦ 'Slow progress is still progress. I may not have all the answers, but I can start putting what I do know into practice and see where that takes me.'

So, if you want to stop procrastinating, you've got to change the narrative in your mind. Instead of thinking you're not good enough for the job or worrying about something going wrong, think about how doing that task could add value to your life and help you feel more fulfilled. This is how you turn procrastination into productivity.

Let's say honesty is one of your values. Having a difficult conversation might be hard, but doing it will help you stay true to your authentic self and honour your values. This will motivate you to be brave enough to speak your mind and be honest to your friend. In the next chapter you'll learn some practical techniques to reframe fear which will come in handy when you're battling procrastination.

PROMISES, PROMISES...

A big part of being confident is keeping the promises we make to ourselves. Every time we tell ourselves we'll take action and we don't, we're breaking the trust we have in ourselves and sending a loud message to the universe that our dreams aren't worthy.

Imagine a situation where you'd told a friend you'd help them move house, but every time they invited you to come over and help, you gave them one excuse after the other. Would that friend ever trust you again? Probably not, because when it mattered you didn't show up and you sent a loud message that you were unreliable, and we all know we don't have confidence in unreliable people.

In the same way, when we break the promises we've made to ourselves, we are sending our subconscious the message that we are unreliable and can't be trusted. This fosters a lack of confidence and leads to further inaction and procrastination. If we don't trust ourselves, we won't bet on ourselves, won't believe in our capabilities and definitely won't unlock our full potential. 'I'll do it tomorrow' isn't just a casual phrase to throw around, because say that enough times and before you know it, it's been five years and you still haven't started.

A big part of being confident is keeping the promises we make to ourselves.

If you feel that you've broken the trust with yourself, take steps to rebuild it, just as you would any other relationship. Start by making smaller promises to yourself that you can keep, show compassion, check in with yourself, stay true to your authentic self and honour your values. It will take time, but stay committed, because it's you and you for the rest of your life, so learning to trust yourself should be your number one priority.

So, as you can see, there's a science behind procrastination. You're not lazy, you're not lacking talent, you're not a bum; your negative thoughts are just running you, so you need to turn things around and align the work you have to do and build powerful habits that keep you moving forward.

And that's exactly what we're covering next.

TURNING PROCRASTINATION INTO PRODUCTIVITY

In the past two years, productivity has become quite a loaded word that has either made people feel really bad about themselves or super self-righteous. I'm sure you've all experienced the productivity wars during lockdown, where it seemed that if you didn't write a book, bake banana bread or start an online course, you were a complete failure. (I did none of those, btw.) Our goal-obsessed culture has defined productivity as 'non-stop hustle and over-achievement'. If you're ticking boxes, you must be productive. I'll be the first to admit my former obsession with ticking boxes. I would put something that was already done on my to-do list just so I could experience the satisfaction of ticking it off.

This view of productivity is a tricky one, though, because when you're 'productive', you feel great and energised, as if you're winning in life, and when you're not, you feel worthless, hopeless, a waste of space... The list goes on. It's so exhausting to hook your worth onto your productivity levels. Similarly to when you're trying to start a new habit, don't let falling short make you feel like you're not good enough to make a change.

You're a human, not a machine. Your worth isn't based on your ability to produce work, your worth is tied to your existence.

#CAKIMantra

The mere fact that you're alive and breathing means you matter.

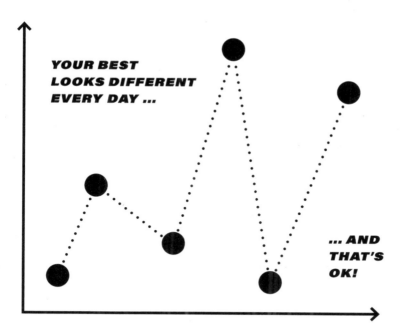

YOUR BEST
LOOKS DIFFERENT
EVERY DAY ...

... AND
THAT'S
OK!

YOU'RE A HUMAN, NOT A MACHINE.

YOUR WORTH ISN'T BASED ON YOUR ABILITY TO PRODUCE WORK, YOUR WORTH IS TIED TO YOUR EXISTENCE.

#CAKIMantra

DEFINE PRODUCTIVITY ON YOUR OWN TERMS

Remember that I said that part of being Confident and Killing It was knowing what societal rules to accept and reject? Well, this is one of them. Productivity doesn't have to mean doing excessive work to the point of burnout. You can redefine it in a way that works for you. I'd like to invite you to choose a new definition, one that is based on spending your time doing what matters to you.

$$\frac{DOING\ WHAT\ MATTERS}{TIME\ SPENT} = PRODUCTIVITY$$

It's not about the quantity of boxes you're ticking, but the quality of the activity you're doing. Does it honour your values? Does it lead to real growth and progress? Does it contribute to your overall wellbeing and fulfilment?

Another thing I love about this definition is that 'doing what matters' looks like different things to different people. So no one gets to 'show you up', because you make the rules. Doing what matters will also look like different things in different seasons.

So productivity can look like:

○   Rest and relaxation.

○   Setting boundaries.

○   Turning off your phone to focus.

○   Taking action on your goals.

○   Clearing out your inbox.

○   Prioritising your tasks.

○   Going on holiday.

○   Having a bubble bath.

○   Netflix and chilling.

○   Running errands.

○   Going through the mail.

○   Getting together with your colleagues to brainstorm
     solutions.

○   Sacrificing going out to meet your deadlines.

○   Spending time with people you love.

○   Asking for help and delegating.

And the list goes on and on. This definition of productivity also allows you to maintain a good work–life integration, because you can tap into your inner wisdom and prioritise what your body and mind need at that specific time. Notice I said work–life *integration* and not work–life *balance*. In episode 20 of the *Confident and Killing It* podcast I sat down with my iconic

Productivity doesn't have to mean doing excessive work to the point of burnout.

mother, Adenike Ogunlesi, who raised three children while building an incredible garment and retail business and hiring over 200 people in Nigeria, which is ranked 131/190 on the ease of business scale. When we were talking about how to 'do it all', she explained about how she swapped work–life balance for work–life integration. When we think of balance, we think of a 50/50 scale. We're striving to have equal work and equal play, which in reality is impossible. We work five days a week and have a two-day weekend, so the scales are already against us. Work–life integration feels more like a braid: we weave different aspects of our life together to make a single thread. A little bit of work, then some play, then some adventure, then some work, then some wellness, and so on and so forth. That's what productivity can look like too.

Slight caution: this definition of productivity based on spending your time doing what matters to you does require a certain level of self-awareness and discipline. If you have a deadline looming and you spend your day resting and watching Netflix, only to leave yourself with two hours to do five hours' worth of work, that's not productive! If you're falling behind on deadlines and commitments, then you probably need some tough love and focus to get things done. On the other hand, when you are feeling in control and on top of things, you can slow down a bit and turn up the fun.

FIND YOUR FLOW

If you want to be productive, pay attention to what gives you energy and what drains your energy. You can do this by making a list of all the tasks you have to carry out in the day and then writing down how you felt during and after the day in your planner, journal or digital task management board. Once you track your energy levels over time, you can prioritise doing more of what gives you energy, because that will lead to an optimum state of flow. Flow is a state of utter blissful immersion in the present moment. When you're in the flow, you are doing deep-thinking work, you lose track of time and you are fully immersed.

The second letter in the PERMA model, the five pillars of wellbeing designed by positive psychologists, is 'E' for 'Engagement'. As humans, we have a natural inclination to busyness, because when we're not doing anything we tend to feel bored and useless, so working gives us a sense of worthiness. However, as I explained above, the key is not to be busy doing work you couldn't care less about. Real productivity is being engaged in work that truly absorbs and inspires us. That's when we're likely to fulfil our own unique potential.

In *Daring Greatly*, Brené Brown says, 'We don't have to be perfect, just engaged and committed to aligning values with action.'

Perfection isn't the goal, feeling alive is. Aligning your actions with the things that matter to you and to your strengths is what *really* makes you feel confident, productive, successful and valuable. It's also my number one tip for balancing a full-time job and side hustle. Having a full-time job that supports the skills, knowledge and passions you need for your side hustle will help you stay in the flow. For example, I used all the knowledge I was gaining on behaviour change, content production and partnerships management from my job at Girl Effect to build Confident and Killing It, and I used the insights from my online community to support my work at Girl Effect, which was a big advantage when it came time for a promotion. Aligning the two things really set me apart and got me motivated.

When you log off from a long day of work that you've hated every moment of, your energy is drained and you're probably feeling quite emotional and demoralised, so all you want to do is switch off. It's difficult to spend your evenings and weekends building a business when you're unfulfilled for eight hours every day. You're also more likely to achieve your goals when your brain is in a positive state. So if you want to be more productive working on your side hustle, find a full-time job that energises you during the day, so you can maintain momentum at night.

Now, some people are able to use hating their job or current situation as motivation to work harder, and I agree we sometimes have to do work we don't really like because it contributes to something bigger and gets us closer to where we want to be. Perhaps you might need to take a role you're not so excited about at your dream company just so you can get your foot in the door and apply for something else later. Maybe you hate exercising, but you realise how crucial moving your body is

Perfection isn't the goal, feeling alive is.

for your physical and mental health. Sacrificing short-term happiness for long-term gain can be worth it. But being stuck doing work you hate that isn't a means to an end is not beneficial for your growth or your soul.

FOCUS ON YOUR OWN LANE

Comparison feels a lot like driving a car and looking everywhere but ahead of you. It generates productivity guilt. Let's say you wake up at 9 a.m. and go on Instagram and see someone has been up since 6 a.m. and gone to the gym already. You start feeling guilty that you're not working hard enough and worry that you're going to get left behind.

When you define productivity on your own terms, someone else being at the gym while you're having a lie-in has nothing to do with you. Your body needs a lie-in, so that's what you'll do. When your body needs exercise, you'll do that. Rest is essential, not a

Comparison is the biggest driver of low self-esteem and it will either make you feel superior or inferior to other people, and none of those things are healthy.

luxury (we'll dive into this in Chapter 9). Remember, someone else working while you're resting doesn't make you lazy or a failure.

Comparison is the biggest driver of low self-esteem and it will either make you feel superior or inferior to other people, and none of those things are healthy. It's important to remember that your productivity isn't good or bad in relation to what someone else has achieved, just good or bad in relation to you and your own goals.

LOCK IN SMALL WINS TO GAIN MOMENTUM AND BE CONSISTENT

Talent is cool, but consistency is what really takes you over the finish line. One hour studying for an exam is better than ten hours never. Thirty minutes of exercise twice a week is better than one hour never. When you have a big mountain to climb, break it down into baby steps and focus on winning the day. One good day and another and another lead to a good week. One good week and another and another lead to a good month. One good month and another and another lead to a good year. You get the picture. A lot of the time we procrastinate because the task feels so big and overwhelming, we disqualify ourselves before we've even attempted it. Focusing on the baby steps and taking each day as it comes breaks the task down into bite-size pieces that we might feel less resistance towards.

Just win today.

That's my mantra whenever I'm working on a challenging project that could get overwhelming.

CONFIDENT AND KILLING IT IN ACTION

Joanne, a French member of the Confident and Killing It Academy, had a goal to get better at self-promotion and be more visible to her clients. She had set this goal many times before but never quite got there because she had never really taken the time to break it down, overcome the fear, change her mindset and build her confidence. She was just diving straight into the goal, focusing on the end result without taking the necessary first steps to overcome the mental hurdles, and as a result she was giving up easily when the fear creeped in.

After she joined the Academy, learnt about the Just Win Today mindset and started tracking her wins, she re-strategised.

HERE'S WHAT HER NEW PLAN LOOKED LIKE:

Step 1 – Take courses and attend workshops and listen to podcasts in the Confident and Killing It academy to build my confidence and overcome fear of self-promotion.

Step 2 – Connect with my why and align the task with my values. What's my intention behind becoming more visible online? Have a clear vision of the bigger picture.

Step 3 – Take baby steps that will compound into a big win over time. Commit to a twenty-eight-day challenge and post one video of me speaking on social media everyday.

Step 4 – Focus my energy on being proud of myself for keeping the promise I made to myself and enjoy the process instead of being overwhelmed by having to do this for twenty-eight days straight.

Instead of feeling stressed by the need to grow her account, get better at speaking on camera and self-promote all at the same time, she started with winning each day by simply showing up! After a month of consistently doing this, she experienced results beyond what she had originally expected and hasn't looked back since.

In his book *Atomic Habits*, James Clear says it's usually small daily changes that, over time, create big transformational shifts. This is exactly what Joanne experienced. So when you're procrastinating, start by doing *one thing* that will take you *just one step* closer to your goal. Once you get started, you'll build momentum and make progress. For many of us, motivation actually comes once we start, not before. Seeing ourselves making progress fuels us to keep going, because we know our effort isn't in vain and a reward is just round the corner.

Another **#CAKIMantra** that helps me celebrate small wins is this:

Slow progress is still progress.

In our instant gratification world, procrastination can creep in when we're not seeing the progress we expected, so we lose momentum and start deprioritising what's important. 'Slow progress is still progress' ditches perfectionism and allows us to embrace the journey rather than obsess over the finish line.

TURN YOUR TO-DO LIST INTO A GET TO-DO LIST

If your to-do list gives you anxiety because it just feels like you have so much to do in so little time, then use this powerful technique to align it with your values and reframe it from activities you *have* to do to activities you *get* to do. I don't *have* to record a podcast episode, I *get* to record an episode and impact someone's life in a positive way. I don't *have* to meditate, I *get* to meditate and take care of my mind, body and soul.

CONFIDENCE CHECK-IN: ACHIEVING DAILY FULFILMENT

Making this mindset shift from 'I should do this' to 'I'm grateful for the opportunity to do this' will be a game-changer for your productivity.

Using the list of values you created in Chapter 1, create three to five buckets of your top values and then categorise your to-do list into those buckets. See the example below:

IMPACT	CREATIVITY	WELLNESS
Record podcast episode	Research content ideas & design posts	Exercsie x2
Prep for webinar with Google	Design presentation templates	One hour of reading in the morning
Send off invoices	Plan outfits for upcoming events	Go for an afternoon walk in the park
Prep for coaching session		Mini spa day with friend

For me, this method was a great way to still be ambitious while prioritising my wellness. With this technique, an afternoon walk in the park is just as valuable as prepping for a workshop.

CONFIDENT AND KILLING IT

SLOW PROGRESS IS STILL PROGRESS.

#CAKIMantra

MANAGE YOUR TIME AND PRIORITISE YOUR TASKS

The American Psychological Association says that switching from unrelated tasks (also known as Context Switching) cuts down our productivity levels.[3] So if you want to get into a state of flow, it's better to time block and group similar activities together, so you can save your energy and limit the number of distractions that get in the way. Here's an example of how I time block one of my work days:

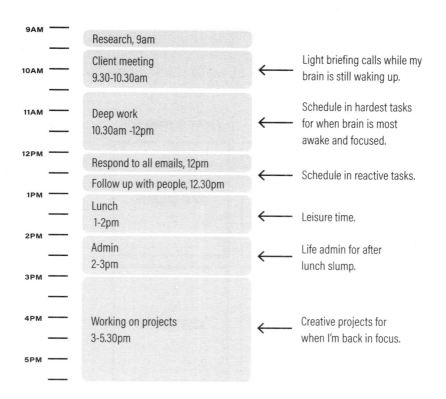

9AM	Research, 9am	
10AM	Client meeting 9.30-10.30am	← Light briefing calls while my brain is still waking up.
11AM	Deep work 10.30am -12pm	← Schedule in hardest tasks for when brain is most awake and focused.
12PM	Respond to all emails, 12pm Follow up with people, 12.30pm	← Schedule in reactive tasks.
1PM	Lunch 1-2pm	← Leisure time.
2PM	Admin 2-3pm	← Life admin for after lunch slump.
3PM	Working on projects 3-5.30pm	← Creative projects for when I'm back in focus.
4PM		
5PM		

The Eisenhower Matrix is a really great tool for deciding how to prioritise tasks. Prioritise what is urgent and important, delegate what is urgent but not important, schedule in a time to do it if it is important but not urgent, and if it's not urgent and not important then remove it completely from your to-do list.

Getting organised really sets you up for success and boosts your confidence. When you see yourself making progress, you are more likely to believe you have what it takes to turn your dreams into a reality and so you take action.

Grouping tasks is a great way to make them feel more manageable and get the ball rolling. Don't forget your environment also plays an important part in being productive and following through with new habits. Set yourself up for success by making sure your environment supports the new changes you're trying to make.

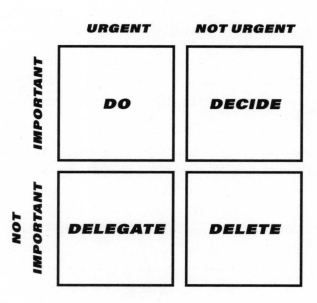

Self-compassion is a much more powerful motivation tool than self-criticism.

So, hey, you did it! You stayed on for the ride and you've got through the first turbulent part where you've had to look at yourself in the mirror and be honest with yourself regarding your relationship with perfectionism and procrastination. This chapter has woken you up to the choice you have to let go of beliefs and rules that sabotage you and choose to take on new ways of thinking and living that will elevate you and unlock your best self. The next time you feel the need to hide behind perfectionism to avoid criticism, judgement and shame, remember that the goal in life isn't to be liked by everyone, but to be your true authentic self. Some people will like it and some people won't, but that's *their* problem, not yours.

When it comes to turning procrastination into productivity, be aware of the connection between your thoughts, feelings and actions. Make sure you know why the tasks you do are important to you and how they align with your values.

Finally, self-compassion is a much more powerful motivation tool than self-criticism. Both may get you to your final destination, but using self-criticism and being hard on yourself as a form of motivation feels like going through life with a tonne of bricks on your back. It's painful, exhausting and straight-up bad vibes. Whereas self-compassion feels like a burst of love and encouragement, it puts a spring in your step and forms a very strong foundation for you to start betting on yourself.

5

STARTING TO BET ON YOURSELF

Fear is a negative thought of something in the future that hasn't happened yet. We think, 'What if I mess up? What if they laugh at me? What if they don't love me? What if I fail? What if my dream never comes true? What if they ghost me?' Then, as we begin to visualise everything going wrong, our body gets tight and we feel nervous, anxious and worried, and then we retreat. Sound familiar?

In the last few chapters, we've looked at how you can get better at believing in your worth, your capability and not waiting to be perfect before you start. Once you overcome the mental hurdle of perfection and procrastination and start taking baby steps, after a while, as you gain momentum, you will get to a point in your life where you have to make a big decision. Maybe it's time to overcome your commitment issues and allow yourself to be loved, or it's time to make the leap from a full-time job to your side hustle, or even leave everything you know behind and go travelling for a year. Whatever it is, you've been going along on your journey and now you're at a cliff with no bridge over the chasm. You can either take a leap of faith and jump, or settle down at the edge, never making it to the other side. If you've been choosing to settle at the edge of the cliff up until now, then wakey, wakey, it's time to pack up that tent and get going. The next few pages are about to set you free and give you the courage you need to start betting on yourself.

THE POWER IN FACING YOUR FEARS

Let's start with why fear seems to have so much power over us. Fear feels so paralysing. It feels heavy, it feels overwhelming, it slows us down to the point of no action.

Like most negative emotions we tend to avoid, fear can be useful and it can be crippling. Fear of getting burnt stops us from putting our hand in the fire. Fear of death stops us from being too relaxed in dangerous situations. Fear acts as a signal when our brain feels we're in danger.

Fear has saved many lives, but it has also killed many dreams. A lot of people think, 'If I feel afraid, that's a sign that maybe I shouldn't do it.' And in some situations that makes sense: feeling afraid of heights stops us from going too close to the edge and falling off a tall building by mistake. But when it comes to goals, dreams and opportunities that help unlock our potential, we can't take that approach.

Confidence isn't an absence of fear. Every single one of us, no matter how confident we may look on the outside, has felt afraid at some point in our life.

CONFIDENT AND KILLING IT IN ACTION

Take my dear friend Fisayo Longe, founder of Kai Collective, for example. After failing university, she decided to go all in with her love for fashion and take a bet on herself by starting her own label. And even after overcoming that initial fear of going out on her own, she's had to fight the fear over and over again as her business grows.

I asked her if she had experienced any fear before she dropped the iconic Gaia print and dress in 2020 that changed her life and her business and shook up the whole fashion industry. Here's what she said: 'At the time I launched it, the market was so minimalist, there wasn't anything like it, and I thought maybe it was too busy and too chaotic. I thought people wouldn't get it... And what's really interesting is that even after I dropped the first dress in purple and it did really well, the fear was still there. Then I created a new colour wave in orange, and the night before it dropped, I called my friend, saying, "No one is going to like this colour, I shouldn't have done this colour, it was a mistake, I've messed it all up," but then that did really well too. So yeah, the fear and anxiety never really go away.'

That Gaia collection generated about £400,000 worth of sales in 2020 alone and has been worn by numerous celebrities like Gabrielle Union, Saweetie and Michaela Coel, been featured in fashion magazines all over the world and sparked a resurgence of bold colourful prints in the fashion industry. Simply put, it has been a global phenomenon. Imagine if Fisayo had let the fear win and never launched it? For the first couple of years Kai was a loss-making brand, but as she reflected on her journey, she said, 'Even at my lowest, I believed in myself.'

Fear is often a battle we have to face every day. The key difference between people who reach their potential and those who don't is that they feel the fear, master it and keep moving forward. They see fear as a natural part of being human. So it's less about whether you feel afraid or not and more about how you respond to the fear when it arrives. Do you retreat or, like Fisayo, do you push past it?

In her book *Everything Is Figureoutable*, Marie Forleo says, 'Fear is not the enemy, waiting to feel afraid is.' Beating yourself up or being mean to yourself for feeling afraid isn't helpful. Fear is normal and it's OK to feel afraid. Your feelings are valid. What's not OK is to let fear rob you of the rich and abundant life you deserve.

When we experience fear, it feels so real, so heavy, so overwhelming. It's so real that we are 100 per cent sure that what we're afraid of is going to happen, and no one can convince us otherwise. But all this time it's just one big 'what if', one big possibility that may or *may not* happen. Fear tricks us into believing that the worst outcome is the only outcome. The truth is, it's not. There are many more possible outcomes that we need to acknowledge and

The key difference between people who reach their potential and those who don't is that they feel the fear, master it and keep moving forward.

explore, however much fear will try and persuade us otherwise. Rehearsing the worst outcome over and over again guarantees the worst outcome. Why? Because that's what we've channelled all our energy and attention into. Remember what you learned in Chapter 3? Energy flows where attention goes.

Fear of failure often leads to inaction, and inaction guarantees failure, because no decision or progress has been made. So if you keep thinking, 'What if I fail, what if I fail, what if I fail?', you are 100 per cent going to fail, because the fear of failure stops you from even trying.

You will fail if you do nothing. If you try, you might fail, *but* you might succeed. Failure is a possibility, not a certainty. By not trying you are giving yourself a 0 per cent chance of achieving your goal.

✦ Now what's the best way to find out what the outcome will be in the future? *Give yourself a chance.*

✦ What's the best way to find out if people will buy your product or service? *Put it up for sale.*

✦ What's the best way to find out if you'll get a promotion? *Apply for it.*

✦ What's the best way to find out if you will enjoy taking a trip on your own? *Book it.*

✦ What's the best way to find out if that person is right for you? *Go on the date.*

The only way to find out what the future holds is to take action now.

The only way to find out what the future holds is to take action now. Fear stops you from trying, fear keeps you from growing, it holds you back in life. When you don't grow or make progress, your potential begins to die.

It's like putting a plant in a dark room with no light or water and expecting it to thrive. If you want to thrive in life, if you want to become the person of your dreams, you have to live in the light. You have to lean into the positive possibilities of your life rather than letting fear keep you in a vicious cycle of rehearsing the worst possible outcome and not even trying.

The three biggest fears I see in the women I've coached and spoken to are:

○   Fear of failure: 'What if it all goes wrong?'

○   Fear of inadequacy: 'What if I'm not good or capable enough?'

○   Fear of judgement: 'What if no one likes or understands the real me?'

Imposter syndrome also feeds off fear. You're afraid to fail, because you think if you do, other people will think you're a fraud or a fake. You're afraid to ask for help, because you think other people will think you're weak and don't really know what you're doing. You're afraid to put yourself up for opportunities, because you think if you don't have all the answers, people will think you're not smart enough to have the opportunities. All of these fears are linked with our deepest human desires to succeed, feel seen, feel heard and know that we matter.

Again, it's totally natural that your biggest fears are in direct correlation with the things you want the most. In a boxing match a heavyweight fights a heavyweight, not a lightweight. They want to go after their match, they want the big boys. In the same way, your biggest fears and doubts go after your biggest dreams and desires. They go after the things you want the most.

Once you become aware of that, you'll stop seeing fear as a sign to retreat and instead you'll see it as a sign that you *must* move forward. You'll begin to ask yourself, 'What else could this mean? What other possibilities exist?' For example, what if asking for help wasn't a sign of weakness and actually was a sign of being a strategic thinker and good collaborator? What if failure was a stepping stone or a launch pad to success rather than a sign that you weren't good enough?

We need to stop seeing failure as a wholly and irreversible negative experience. If you're going to be afraid of failure, then be afraid of never starting and missing out on your life. That's where the real failure is. If you bet on yourself and try something new and it doesn't work out, you now have more knowledge, because you know what works and what doesn't and can make better decisions next time, which in all honesty is a win.

In the *The War of Art: Break Through the Blocks and Win Your Inner Creative Battles*, author Steven Pressfield explains you will always feel resistance when you're moving from a lower sphere to a higher sphere in life. What that resistance means is open for interpretation. You can translate it as fear and a sign to retreat or you can translate it as an obstacle you need to push past or a battle you need to win in order to reach a new level of your life.

Now, if you're reading this book, it's very likely that you want to win that battle against fear. That goal is absolutely possible, and I want nothing more than to see you winning the battle and taking action so you can live a life you deserve and not a life that has been robbed of opportunity by the lies of fear.

So my question to you is: How long are you going to keep believing the lies? How long are you going to let fear mess you around and run things in your life? Aren't you tired of feeling stuck and overwhelmed? I think it's time to master fear once and for all.

REFRAMING FEAR

Confidence isn't an absence of fear, confidence is feeling the fear but doing it anyways.

#CAKIMantra

Here's a Reframing Fears Technique (RFT). It'll help you break down your fears so they no longer have power over you. By the

CONFIDENCE ISN'T AN ABSENCE OF FEAR, CONFIDENCE IS FEELING THE FEAR BUT DOING IT ANYWAYS.

#CAKIMantra

time you have gone through these six steps, the fear shouldn't feel so scary anymore and you should begin to manage it instead of letting it manage you.

STEP 1:

NAME THE FEAR

What's making you feel afraid or anxious? You've got to name it because you can't master what you don't first acknowledge. Acknowledging fear instead of avoiding it will allow you to work through it quicker. It's important not to group your fears; break them down into single sentences so you can tackle one at a time. Big fears feel scary, mini fears can be more manageable. One of my clients, Anita, was thinking about taking the leap to become a full-time entrepreneur and her fear was 'what if I'm not successful?' That fear was quite broad and had many other fears within it, like 'What if I let my parents down?' or 'What if I can't network enough and find clients?' Always try to break down your fear on a granular level so you can really see what's going on.

Acknowledging fear instead of avoiding it will allow you to work through it quicker.

STEP 2:

WHAT CAN YOU BE GRATEFUL FOR IN THIS CHALLENGING SITUATION?

This might sound like a strange question, because we're not really taught to be grateful for fear, we're taught to run from it or avoid it, but gratitude has a powerful way of spinning things around. In coaching we call this reframing. In Anita's situation, even though her parents were worried about her quitting her job, she was grateful they were at least invested in her future and wanted to see her do well. Even though she was afraid of letting them down, she was grateful they cared.

Being in this situation added value to her life, because she would learn that sometimes disappointing others in order not to disappoint yourself was OK. She would learn how to defend her dreams to people who didn't get her vision. This fear would encourage her to have an open and vulnerable conversation with her parents, which would inevitably bring them closer.

When you reframe fear and look at how it can add value to your life, it makes it less scary. Seeing fear as a challenge that could help her grow as an individual made it more palatable to Anita.

If you're afraid of quitting your job to start your business, you can be grateful that at least you have a business idea worth pursuing. If you're afraid of being ghosted by somebody, you can be grateful for the clarity that that person definitely was not right for you and reclaim your time. If you're afraid people might judge you, you can be grateful that you'll be able to really see those judgemental people for who they are and go and find a more supportive community. If you're afraid of failure, you can be grateful that in the process, you will learn what doesn't work so you can focus on what does. You can embrace the opportunity to build your resilience and practise the art of not giving up (which is bound to come in handy later on in your life). Gratitude has a powerful way of turning fear on its head.

STEP 3:

WHAT WILL HAPPEN IF YOU KEEP FOCUSING ON THE NEGATIVE ENERGY?

A lot of people focus on the action they need to take being scary and never look into what the consequences are if they decide not to move forward. But avoiding failure doesn't give you success. Avoiding depression doesn't lead to happiness. If you keep thinking, 'What if I mess up?', you'll feel tense and anxious, you'll feel like a failure, and what will happen as a result? You won't take action and will stay in your comfort zone. What happens when you stay in your comfort zone? You don't grow. What happens when you don't grow? You feel unfulfilled, you feel stuck, you lack motivation and ambition. What happens when you feel unfulfilled? You begin to hate your life, hate yourself and feel depressed. It's a long movie on a downward spiral. The next time you feel afraid, play the full movie out in your head and see if that's the path you want your life to take. Probably not.

In Anita's example, her fear of letting her parents down would mean staying in a job that didn't fulfil her. Feeling unfulfilled would lead to being demotivated and sad and lacking ambition. She'd most likely procrastinate, feel a failure and live a very average life with no real growth trajectory. Her lack of growth, ambition and success would eventually lead to disappointing her parents who, at the end of the day, wanted to see her well and thriving.

So, as you can see, when you focus on fear, that is exactly what you end up getting. Fear of failure leads to inaction, and inaction guarantees failure, because no progress is made. The consequences of giving into fear and retreating, faaaar outweigh the momentary pain you might feel by pushing through the pain and learning to master it.

HOW WOULD YOU RATHER THINK, FEEL OR ACT? DESCRIBE YOUR IDEAL SITUATION IN THE PRESENT TENSE

If fear is what you don't want, let's focus on what you *do* want! Anxiety is what we feel when we are worried, tense or afraid, particularly about things that are about to happen, or which we think could happen in the future. Grounding yourself by focusing on what you would rather be thinking and feeling (in the present moment) instead of worrying about what you don't want to happen (in the future) can really help calm your nerves.

Take a moment to articulate what you would rather be thinking, feeling and doing instead of the fear you are feeling. Park the fear to one side, a bit of distance from the emotion can help, and write down all the good things you actually want. Write it as if they were already in your life. Anita wrote:

> *I am making my parents proud by being someone who can bet on themselves and turn an idea into a reality. My parents see the value and impact my idea could have and encourage me to pursue it even if they don't fully understand it.*

If you suffer from social anxiety for example, instead of seeing yourself being awkward and alone at a social event, try and see yourself confident, comfortable and thriving. See yourself making meaningful connections with people. When the nerves start to creep in, challenge the negative self-talk and get back to visualising the outcome you want.

We all feel a small amount of anxiety throughout our life, but if your feelings of anxiety are intense and long-lasting, then please see a medical professional about it.

STEP 5:

WHAT CAN YOU DO TODAY TO MOVE CLOSER TO YOUR IDEAL SITUATION?

The magic is in the baby steps. In the very first step. So start with just one small step. Confident and Killing It started with a one-minute video on Instagram. After one video, I made another one, and another and another, and four years later it's a successful company and I'm writing this book. It was my consistent baby steps over the years that led to this moment.

If you make a commitment to yourself to do one thing every day that takes you closer to your goal, you will move faster than the people on the side-lines waiting for their big break. Start small and gain momentum instead of paralysing yourself by focusing on all the big things that need to be done. Plus the more you do something, the less fear you begin to feel about it.

For Anita this looked like:

1. Sitting her parents down for that open and honest conversation.

2. Finalising her business plan so she could show it to her parents with confidence.

3. Doing two hours of research to come up with example use cases.

Confidence is a practice, and like anything we practise, we get better over time. As you go through life, new fears will spark new opportunities to build confidence. Sometimes courage will just kick in, we will jump off the cliff and take a bet that we'll fly. Other times mastering fear is a bit of a slow burner. Take whatever approach works for you, as long as you're moving forward.

STEP 6:

HOW CAN YOU BOUNCE BACK IF YOUR FEAR BECOMES A REALITY?

In this final step, it's essential to reconnect with the strengths you identified in Chapter 1. If you do lose your job, what do you have within you to help you bounce back? Are you resilient? Are you creative? Are you hardworking? Creating a bounce back plan will help you feel more confident taking the risk. By internal resources I mean looking at what strengths in your strengths log you can kick into action and also exploring past memories of when you've overcome a similar fear. Figure out what strategies you used and then apply them again. For example, if you overcame the fear to move to another country or go solo travelling, you can apply the same approach when it comes to overcoming the fear of starting a business – in both situations you left your comfort zone to venture into the unknown. Then depending on what the fear is about think of external support systems you can lean on like loved ones, mentors, community groups and learning programs. Don't let fear make you feel helpless. Remember the **#CAKIMantra** 'Everything you need to win in life is already within you.'

For Anita, if she did end up disappointing her parents she could use her determination and drive, which we identified as her top strengths, to not give up even if she failed the first time. She could use her communication skills to have an honest conversation with her parents. She could use her confidence to not let other people's opinions get in the way of her dreams. She could also find a business mentor to help her rethink her strategy. As you know, when I thought about potentially failing as an entrepreneur, I remembered that my favourite word was 'unstoppable' because I knew when I got hit, I would always get back up. As long as I'm alive, I will never give up on myself. This strength gave me the security and courage to take the leap, because even if my worst nightmare happened, which it actually did due to the pandemic, I would find a way to get back up again. For external resources my family, my community and listening to business podcasts were a lifeline for me.

When we feel afraid, we often doubt that we have what it takes to make it through the fear, but is that really true? I know fear feels like a big scary monster, but you are not a small helpless creature that can be swept up easily. *You are bigger than your fear.* If you take a moment to look at the strengths inside you, you will clearly see that everything you need to win in life is *already* inside you. You just have to wake up to it.

Failure is something we fear so much but we aren't our failures.

Failure is an event. It's something that happens to you, it's not who you are.

#CAKIMantra

FAILURE IS AN EVENT.

IT'S SOMETHING THAT HAPPENS TO YOU, IT'S NOT WHO YOU ARE.

#CAKIMantra

So you can *experience* failure but you can never *be* a failure. Failure has a start and end date, so don't let it define your whole life. It's only a shameful dead end if you allow it to be.

When you're confident, you define and redefine your life over and over again because you know your life belongs to *you*, and *you* make the rules. You can use this mindset when it comes to failure. You can learn to redefine it in a way that doesn't make you run from it but embrace it with open arms, because it leads to something bigger and better. So, don't let fear bully you and make you feel small. Tap into your inner greatness, visualise the outcome you actually want, create a bounce back plan and take baby steps.

You only have one life, and this is it. Don't take it for granted. The world needs you. The world needs your ideas. The world needs your light. You can **F**ace **E**verything **A**nd **R**un or you can **F**ace **E**verything **A**nd **R**ise. The choice is yours.

You can *experience* failure but you can never *be* a failure.

THE GOLDEN RULES WHEN YOU FEEL LIKE GIVING UP

Mastering fear is something we have to do over and over again. Imagine if all we had to do was overcome one fear and then it was smooth sailing after that. That would be cute, but unfortunately very unrealistic. When I overcame my fear of becoming a full-time entrepreneur, I thought the fact that I had overcome my biggest worries meant that nothing else would get in my way. Girl, was I wrong. Once you start to bet on yourself and take risks, you will make progress but you will still come across hurdles. There will be some days when you feel like giving up because life just feels so hard. When that happens, remember these golden rules:

REMEMBER YOUR WHY

Think about why the goal matters to you. What's the bigger picture? How does this goal give you fulfilment and have a bigger impact on the world around you?

The fourth pillar of the five pillars of the PERMA wellbeing model is 'M' for 'Meaning'. Studies have shown it is very important to feel that the work we do is consistent with our personal values and beliefs. From day to day, *if we believe our work is worthwhile, we feel a general sense of motivation and confidence that we are using our time and our abilities for good.* There is also evidence to show that people who belong to a community and pursue shared goals are happier than people who don't.[1]

So, if you feel the work you're doing isn't in alignment with your purpose, values and beliefs, you will give up easily when things get hard, because there's no sense of direction, no vision and certainly no motivation. This is why creating your Power Circle was one of the first concepts we explored. When you're living in alignment with your strengths, passions and values, betting on yourself and seeing the journey through are much easier.

After I had been quietly volunteering behind the scenes as a youth leader and overcoming my fear of public speaking in a place where no one knew me, I reached the point in my journey where it was time to stop hiding and start sharing my knowledge and expertise on a bigger scale and in particular in front of people who knew me. I remember the fear I felt before I posted my first ever inspirational Instagram video. My negative thoughts told me I would get laughed at and nobody would care. At that moment I was at a crossroads: listen to fear and retreat or post the video. I remembered my 'why' and I asked myself, 'What is more important than the fear you feel?' I began to think of all the young women in my youth group who were struggling with confidence and really needed to hear this message. I thought of a younger Tiwalola who was suffocating under the weight of comparison. Yes, my fear was big and real, but the message in me was more important than the fear I was feeling.

The message in you is more important than the fear you feel.

#CAKIMantra

CONFIDENT AND K...

THE MESSAGE IN YOU IS MORE IMPORTANT THAN THE FEAR YOU FEEL.

#CAKIMantra

So, the next time you feel fearful, anxious or ready to give up, remember your why. Remember *one* person who needs your message, your product or service.

The world needs you.

Your voice, your ideas and your contributions are all bigger than the fear you feel.

REMEMBER BAD SITUATIONS ARE NOT PERMANENT

When things are going wrong, it's hard to see the light at the end of the tunnel. We often feel the bad situation or challenge is permanent and pervasive, but it rarely is. It's often only one area in life that's challenging and not our *whole* life. So try not to generalise or use all or nothing thinking as we talked about in Chapter 2.

More importantly, if you give up in the middle of the storm, you 100 per cent guarantee that your dreams won't come true. So learn to rest, process your emotions and take baby steps instead of giving up completely. Slow progress is better than no progress. Crawling out of a challenge is better than sitting in it feeling helpless. Be grateful for any small improvement and be proud of how far you've come.

A slight word of caution: I don't want to romanticise perseverance, because sometimes giving up is exactly what we need to do.

It's OK to quit when you feel you've completely hit a dead end. There's no shame in that. Blind persistence can lead to a pointless and exhausting quest. Sometimes the mature thing to do is accept your losses and walk away, instead of pouring more time and resources into the situation or person. For example, you might want to consider quitting in some of these circumstances:

○ If you're the only one putting all the energy and effort into a relationship, you'll need to accept you aren't a match and walk away.

○ If the only reason you're staying in a relationship is because you don't know who you are without that person, it's probably time to leave and find true self-love.

○ If pursuing your goal is making you very, very unhappy and you start to hate yourself, it's time to rethink the goal.

○ If the only reason you haven't already quit is because you're worried about what other people will think, it's probably time to quit and prioritise your needs.

○ If the idea of giving up floods you with relief, quitting so you can change paths is a good idea.

Things don't always work out as planned, and if you've tried everything and it's still not working, then it's also OK to give up.

REMEMBER TO SPEAK UP AND ASK FOR HELP WHEN YOU HIT A ROADBLOCK

Asking for help isn't a weakness. Life isn't meant to be lived on your own and, as I mentioned earlier, psychologists have found that working with a group of people to achieve a shared goal really gives our life a sense of meaning. You can be an independent woman and still have a strong support system that you can lean on when you get stuck; the two aren't mutually exclusive. Imposter syndrome will make you feel afraid to ask for help because society has told to us that successful people do it all on their own, but that's a lie. Asking for help when you get stuck doesn't make you a burden, it doesn't mean you're a failure, in actuality it creates opportunities for you to learn and level up. It creates opportunities for you to show those around you that they are needed and valued.

Here's how Rikki and Beckah, UK members of the Confident and Killing It Academy asked for help and got so much more in return:

CONFIDENT AND KILLING IT IN ACTION

Rikki:

Story time I outsourced a task because I had too much on my plate this week. The freelancer tried to overcharge me and at first, I thought 'should I just do it myself?' Then I

paused and reminded myself why I outsourced in the first place. Then the people-pleaser I used to be resurfaced and I thought 'should I just accept their offer?' And I paused again, reminded myself of my worth and value, made my expectations clear to him and he halved the price! Then when he submitted it, I could tell a lot of it was generic and was actually irrelevant to the task and I felt he was taking advantage of me. I paused, allowed myself to cool down, restated my expectations, made it clear that the quality was unacceptable and I wasn't going to accept it and that he needed to revise the whole document. He did and the quality is 1000x better! Was I Confident and Killing It? I think so!

By being brave enough to ask for help, Rikki created the opportunity to also practice other parts of confidence – believing in her worth, asking for what she wants and being unapologetic about her standards. Now she has so many wins and positive moments to remind herself of the next time she's in a challenge.

CONFIDENT AND KILLING IT IN ACTION

Beckah:

I had to give a presentation two weeks ago to my company (100+ people) on identifying and overcoming imposter syndrome, generally and specifically in the industry of advertising which can be a very intense environment. Despite presenting regularly as part of my job, I found myself to be very nervous and wanting to pull out as I'd never shared my personal experiences or advice in such a public forum and wasn't sure how to make it land without sounding self-centred. I opened up to my team about the fear I was feeling and asked for their help. They helped me challenge my self-doubt, reviewed the presentation and reassured me of how powerful it was.

When I presented it to the wider organisation, the response was overwhelming; I received more positive feedback and notes from people who said it made so many things make sense for them than I could have ever imagined.

I feel it had a very positive outcome in that I didn't just help people in my company who had been struggling with these feelings without anyone to relate or talk to openly, but I also helped myself by not being afraid to ask for help when I needed it. My colleagues' support encouraged me to go ahead and the success of it all helped me see that sharing my story (as you always advocated and inspired me to do, Tiwa) made me feel alive and energised in a way I've been searching for for years.

Through her vulnerability and ability to ask for help, Beckah unlocked a new level of fulfilment in her life as she learned first-hand the power of her story. She was known as a confident person who had run many presentations at work before, but she didn't let the fear of looking like a fraud stop her from asking for help when she needed it. Asking for help led to following through with the presentation. Doing the presentation led to increased levels of passion, fulfilment and self-awareness.

Worrying is literally praying for the worst outcome.

Now, many corporations value people who can take the initiative and solve problems, so when you do go and ask for help, make sure you've at least attempted to find a solution. No one has all the answers and no one can do it all on their own, so when things get tough, make sure you have a strong community you can lean on, a group of people that will encourage you to keep going and cheer you on. If you can't ask for help from those around you, then you're in the wrong environment.

Energy flows where attention goes, so if you want less fear, less stress and less self-doubt, focus your energy on the things you want for your life. Don't worry about how you're going to get it, don't worry about whether you'll be able to handle it or not – worrying is literally praying for the worst outcome. Instead visualise and meditate on a positive vision for the future. Every time a fearful thought interrupts that, question it, separate the facts from assumptions and replace the sabotaging thought with a more empowering one. This a process you'll have to repeat in life over and over again.

Much like perfectionism, imposter syndrome is rooted in fear – fear you won't live up to expectations and people will think you're a fraud, fear that you aren't as competent as others perceive you to be and one day they'll find out the truth. According to the *International Journal of Behaviour Science* about 70 per cent of adults will experience imposter syndrome at some point in their life and it's most common when people are going through transitions or new experiences like starting a new school, job or making new connections.[2]

A lack of experience can trigger feelings of fear and inadequacy, and so in those moments, it's essential to remember your transferable skills, remember all your previous accomplishments and use those as motivation to keep going and bet on yourself. A report showed 'women are 55 per cent more likely than men to cite fear of going it alone as a primary reason for not starting a business.'[3] To me, this fear screams, 'Will I be good enough?', 'Do I have what it takes?' And this answer is '*Yes!*', so bet on yourself.

Here's the thing: when you work for someone, your employer owns the job title, but they don't own your skills, knowledge and expertise. Those belong to you. So if you're thinking about leaving your job to start a business, or taking any sort of risk in life, you are rarely starting from an inexperienced place. You don't leave your skills at the door when you hand in your badge on the last day. All of that knowledge and past experience goes with you. And if you are doing something completely new, lean on your ability to Learn and Level Up!

So the next time you're afraid to go into unfamiliar territory, remember who the f*ck you are. In fact, the next time you're afraid to do *anything*, remember who you are and give yourself a chance. You are someone with strengths, you are someone with unique gifts, you are someone who matters, you are someone who has survived 100 per cent of the challenges that have come your way. You might fail, but you might succeed, and you are worthy of taking that bet to see how it goes. You never know how you might surprise yourself.

In the coming chapters we're going to look at how you can get better at internalising your success and keep track of your accomplishments so when fear and imposter syndrome creep in, you remember what you're capable of.

Remember the greatness inside you, because you, sis, are no small thing.

6

LET YOUR BOUNCE BACK BE STRONGER THAN YOUR SETBACK

A big part of confidence that we tend to forget is the impact external circumstances and people can have on it. Yes, confidence is a practice, and yes, it's a lot to do with belief in our abilities. But that belief can be impacted greatly by the environments we find ourselves in as well as situations that are outside our control.

By this point, you've woken up to your authentic self, you've mastered your mindset, you no longer let perfectionism hold you back, you believe in your capabilities and you've taken the leap of faith and followed the golden rules when you've felt like giving up... Even after all this, there will still be setbacks that will knock your confidence. Why? Because no one is 100 per cent confident 100 per cent of the time. Confidence isn't perfection. You will have good days and you will have bad days. Things like rejection, friendship break-ups and receiving negative feedback at work will hurt! No matter how old or confident you are, rejection will always hurt. You could be the most confident person in the world, but if you were in a toxic relationship where you were being put down, manipulated and emotionally abused, you would still lose some of your confidence. So in this chapter I want to help with those moments when your confidence has been knocked and you need to build it back up again.

Being Confident and Killing It isn't about floating through life feeling flawless and untouchable every day. You will get hit and you will get setbacks, but the focus shouldn't be on what happens to you, but on how you respond to what happens to you.

The beautiful thing about confidence being a practice is that if it has been knocked, it can be rebuilt with intention and strategy. Which is what this book is all about!

When bad things happen to you, the lens through which you view them has the power to influence what action you take. Have a look at the kind of perspectives people tend to have in the midst of challenging situations:

VICTIM VIEW	CREATOR VIEW
It's permanent. Life will never be the same again.	It's temporary. It's just a season, it will pass.
Everything is bad.	It's just this one area of my life.
Nothing is in my control. I'm helpless.	Some things might not be in my control, but I'll focus on what I *can* control.
I must be a bad person for all of this to be happening to me. I'm not worthy of good things.	I am always worthy of good things. Sometimes bad things happen to good people.

Victims see situations as permanent, pervasive and out of their control. When they have a negative experience, they discount all their previous successes just to focus on this one negative moment, and they feel defined by it. They accept it as their fate and replay it over and over again in their mind.

Creators, on the other hand, understand that life happens in seasons and that most challenges are temporary. When they have a negative experience, they don't discount all their previous successes, but learn from their mistakes. Instead of feeling helpless, they look for opportunities to move forward.

So, the next time you find yourself in the middle of a storm, take a step back and look at how you're viewing the situation. A victim view leads to a dead end. A creator view gives you hope, and where there is hope, there is the opportunity to move forward and come out the other side stronger than ever.

REBUILDING YOUR CONFIDENCE AFTER IT'S BEEN KNOCKED

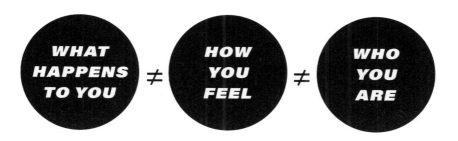

WHAT HAPPENS TO YOU ≠ HOW YOU FEEL ≠ WHO YOU ARE

Here are five keys to coming back stronger once your confidence has been knocked:

1. One negative situation in the past doesn't define your whole lifetime... unless you let it.

Failure, discrimination, rejection and abuse are things that happen *to* us, they are not who we are. You have the option not to carry that weight for the rest of your life. Learn to make peace with your past and wake up to the authority you have to define and redefine your life, over and over again. There is beauty in your strengths and your pain, but try not to get stuck

WHAT HAPPENS
TO YOU,
WHO YOU ARE,
AND HOW YOU FEEL
ARE *THREE*
SEPARATE
THINGS.
YOU ARE NOT YOUR
PAST AND YOU ARE
NOT YOUR
FEELINGS.

#CAKIMantra

in the pain. You deserve to live a trauma-free life, so instead of disqualifying yourself from new beginnings, let your bounce back be stronger than your setback.

This is easier said than done, so if you're struggling to let go of something in the past, don't be afraid to get professional help like therapy. There's no shame in it. Loving yourself enough to get the help you need is a beautiful act of bravery.

2. Your worth is intrinsic – nothing and no one have the power to take it from you.

You matter simply because you exist. Your worth doesn't depend on external things like a degree, money, a job or who you know. Society doesn't give you worth, you are born with it. People don't give you worth, you are born with it. So, when you experience a setback, try not to internalise it as something being wrong with you. Sometimes bad things happen to good people. Regardless of what happens to you, you are always worthy of good things happening to you. People might reject you, they might take away your opportunities, but let the unshakeable worth inside you help your bounce back be stronger than your setback.

3. Your opinion of yourself matters more than what others think of you.

People may have said some mean things to you in the past. Not everyone has the privilege of growing up in a loving and supportive family. You may have been told you weren't good enough, weren't smart enough or there wasn't anything special about you. If you grew up with very little encouragement or have had a very negative teacher,

You deserve to live a trauma-free life, so instead of disqualifying yourself from new beginnings, let your bounce back be stronger than your setback.

partner or manager who has beaten you down, you may be feeling the weight of all those limiting labels. But guess what? If you feel those labels are holding you back in life, you have the power to create a new narrative for yourself. Your opinion of yourself carries more weight than what others think, so make sure you've got good opinions!

This is why it's so important to have good self-esteem, which in all honesty is simply knowing you have worth and liking who you are. You don't have to wait until you have the perfect credit score, body, relationship and job to see the goodness in yourself. It's something you can choose to see every day. Just as you choose what underwear to wear... or not.

One of my British coaching clients and academy members, Juliet, embodied this perfectly when she shared her wins in our weekly wins group:

My big win has actually just happened five minutes ago. For background, I am currently in the process of applying for pupillage (the on-the-job training year you have to do before becoming a fully-fledged barrister). It's incredibly competitive and usually takes people a few years before they get there.

Anyway, I was just speaking to my dad and he basically said that I needed to manage my expectations and I wouldn't get pupillage at my dream places...

Where is the win? It was water off a duck's back. Previously this would have smashed my confidence and ruined my day, but today I thought, 'I can do it! It might be this year, it might be next, or even the year after that ... but I can do it.'

When I first met Juliet, she was struggling to believe she could make a good lawyer because the emotions of having previously failed in business were still weighing heavily on her. Her past failures were blocking her ability to bounce back.

Almost a year after our coaching sessions, not only has she smashed all her bar exams, but she is standing up for herself and defending her worth. Regardless of her past failures, regardless of her insecurities, regardless of the doubt projected onto her, she is choosing to believe in her self-worth, like who she is and own her capabilities.

The lesson here is that there will be people in the world who don't like seeing you shine or be ambitious and they'll try and 'humble' you, but don't let them. No one knows you like you know yourself. No one knows your potential like you do.

The more you love yourself and believe in your capabilities, the less space you have to care about what other people think of you.

#CAKIMantra

So if people try to crush your dreams with their negative words, the best response is to bounce back stronger than ever and kill 'em with consistency, determination and drive.

4. The way people treat you is not a reflection of your self-worth.

If you've ever been discriminated against, you'll know how painful it feels and how easy it is to internalise it and feel there is something wrong with you. One thing I learned very early on is that the way people treat you is not a reflection of your worth, but actually a reflection of their own internal perspective and feelings about themselves. Someone who low-key hates themselves is unable to show you love. A person ghosting you is not a reflection of your worth but a reflection of their lack of respect and poor communication skills. Don't let people who don't matter matter too much.

THE MORE YOU LOVE YOURSELF AND BELIEVE IN YOUR CAPABILITIES, THE LESS SPACE YOU HAVE TO CARE ABOUT WHAT OTHER PEOPLE THINK OF YOU.

#CAKIMantra

5. Rejection doesn't mean you are a reject.

Similarly to failure, rejection is something you experience. It is not your identity. One of the biggest and quickest ways to kill your confidence is to internalise rejection as something being wrong with you. If someone says 'no' to you, it doesn't have to mean you're not good enough. Here are three healthy ways to reframe rejection:

 The timing wasn't right.

When I was getting cancellation emails left, right and centre in the pandemic, it had nothing to do with me. The timing just wasn't right. If you're seeking a work opportunity and get rejected, ask when a good time could be and then try again.

 The opportunity wasn't right.

When one door closes, it's usually because there's something better coming your way. Getting rejected can be a blessing in disguise. Rejection can even be a form of protection and also redirection. Back in 2016 when I was still trying to figure out how to live out my purpose, I managed to get in touch with the headmistress of the Oprah Winfrey Leadership Academy in Johannesburg and pitched a proposal to bring a personal development programme called SHINE to their school. She responded with kind words, but said they already had so much on that the programme wasn't needed at the school. I was distraught, but instead of giving up I channelled my energy into starting my own brand – Confident and Killing It – and started hosting my own events for women and girls. Exactly a year later, I got the opportunity to go to South Africa for work and something nudged me to email the headmistress again. I sent her a video of all the great work I'd been doing since we last spoke and asked if I could come to the school for a day to speak to the girls. She said yes! The first opportunity I pitched wasn't right but I tried again from a different angle and got a yes and to this day it was one of the most unforgettable experiences I've ever had. Don't be disheartened when one door closes, keep knocking until the right one opens.

 You need a bit more time to grow.

No one is perfect and we're all a work in progress so, even though you might feel 100 per cent ready and sure that you can handle something, other people may need to see you succeed and grow a bit more before they have the confidence to bet on you and give you a chance. Again, don't take that personally. Be consistent and keep going, and before you know it, they'll be back again. As I always say:

When people don't give you opportunities, create your own!

#CAKIMantra

Bonus point: You don't need closure to move on.

Looking specifically at friendship break-ups, we never really get the benefit of closure, because the relationship often just dies a slow death. Sometimes there's a fight that shifts the dynamic and you make up, but things aren't the same as before. Other times you just grow into different people with different needs and don't have much in common anymore, or being around you triggers them and they'd rather just exit quietly via the back door than confront you or their insecurities. Regardless of how it happens, it hurts so much! Grieving a loss is sad enough, but grieving a loss when the person is still alive, now that's different.

I believe people are in our life for a reason – and a season. A study has shown we replace half our close friends every seven years,[1] so friendship break-ups are a natural part of our human existence. Some friendships come to an end the same way seasons come and go. People are here for us to experience, not to own or hoard, and sometimes those experiences end earlier than we expected. It is what it is.

Hopefully this perspective will stop you from thinking you're a bad person when things go wrong. If you haven't got closure from a break-up, don't worry, there are still other ways to process things and move on; for example, you could use the 3As from Chapter 2:

○ *Acknowledge* the grief, the anger and sadness. Yes, relationships are amazing, but breakdowns really hurt. Be still for a moment and feel your feelings, because that's the only way to start healing.

○ *Articulate* the specific losses you're experiencing, for example the loss of memories, the loss of the laughter and joy

CONFIDENT AND KILLING IT

WHEN PEOPLE DON'T GIVE YOU OPPORTUNITIES, CREATE YOUR OWN!

#CAKIMantra

that person brought you, the loss of future plans that will never come to pass, the loss of their love and support, etc. Acknowledge that you have lost these things with this specific person, but that you haven't lost all of these things forever. New memories and new friendships can always be made. In her book *I Wish I Knew This Earlier: Lessons on Love*, Toni Tone says, 'When we go through a breakup sometimes it's not the character of the person we miss, it's the routine we had with them. We don't miss the person, we miss having a person.' Well, the good news is that new routines, new memories and new friendships can always be made, so not all losses are complete losses.

○ *Allow* yourself to move forward by forgiving the person, forgiving yourself and then writing down what you most deeply need, even if you don't feel entitled to it. Not from that person specifically, but what you need to flourish and move forward from yourself. If you don't know where to start, the 3As will give you some insight into your needs. Examples could be the need to remind yourself of your value, the need to rekindle your joy, or the need to receive support from the loved ones who are still there.

No matter how old or how confident you are, rejection will always hurt. When you pour your time and energy into something that matters to you and it doesn't work out, it's devastating and totally normal to feel upset and disheartened. Especially when you don't know why it's happened or how you can fix it.

STRENGTHENING YOUR SUPPORT SYSTEM

Yes, Miss Independent, I'm talking to you. You can be the most confident person in yourself, but without the right support system your confidence can only take you so far. Being independent and having a strong support system aren't mutually exclusive. Numerous studies show the impact positive social relationships have on our mental and physical health.[2] Our relationships are such a fundamental part of our wellbeing that they've actually been designated as the third pillar of the PERMA model for achieving ultimate wellness and fulfilment – 'R' for 'Relationships'. Good relationships can reduce our rates of anxiety and depression and lead to higher self-esteem and longevity.[3] Maslow's Hierarchy of Needs, a well-known theory for motivation, states: 'In order to achieve self-actualisation, which is the best version of ourselves that unlocks our full potential, a number of more basic needs must be met such as the need for food, safety: *love and belonging.*[4]

Another persona of imposter syndrome is the Soloist. Soloists are people who prefer to do everything on their own, because they see asking for help as a sign of weakness. They feel the need to work way harder than everyone else so they can measure up to their colleagues, which often leaves them in a place of severe burnout and stress. They tend to believe people will judge them if they don't come across as having all the knowledge and capabilities they need for their job, so they prefer not to ask for support and do it all on their own out of fear. But there's a catch: if you're a soloist, you think you're winning by doing it all on your own, but actually life is hard and when you burn out from

Self-love isn't a substitute for experiencing love and belonging.

overworking and trying to juggle everything, you're less likely to perform at your best and then you end up in a vicious cycle of low self-esteem and imposter syndrome. Not cute.

The truth is there's no award for trying to do it all on your own. As I mentioned earlier, I myself once had the 'It's quicker to do it myself' complex, so I rarely ever delegated or asked for help, but after experiencing burnout from working myself to the ground in order to stay afloat in the pandemic, I had a wake-up moment and learned that it's quicker to get things done with the help of others than it is to struggle all on your own. When we've been knocked and it feels like all hope is lost, having a community that cheers us on can give us a renewed sense of purpose and belonging, which motivates us to get back up again.

Bear in mind there's no one way to do community. It can be online, in-person or a mix of both. It doesn't always have to be a big private member's crew; it can be a few close friends or confidants who care about you.

Humans are social creatures and self-love isn't a substitute for experiencing love and belonging. When we have a good support system, we feel safe enough to take risks and actions that allow us to build confidence. When we feel encouraged by the people around us, we believe in ourselves and feel more capable of succeeding. On the other hand, if we're surrounded by toxic people who don't believe in us and who tear you down with their words, it plants weeds of self-doubt that kill our potential.

Let's look at some clear red and green flags when it comes to relationships, so you'll know the types of people to stay clear of and the ones to surround yourself with.

THREE SIGNS OF UNHEALTHY RELATIONSHIPS THAT WILL KNOCK YOUR CONFIDENCE

The person you're in a relationship with is obsessive:

○ They want to be the centre of attention in your world and at the same time they want you to be their be all and end all. They come across as very possessive.

○ They get upset when you don't prioritise their needs above yours and they often want you to sacrifice your goals and opportunities for them.

○ They aren't that supportive of your wins, as it takes the spotlight away from them.

They're consistently negative:

○ These kinds of people often sow doubts in your mind about yourself and your abilities. They say really mean things to you when they're angry and use their words as a weapon to tear you down.

○ They belittle you and tell stories or jokes at your expense. They're very critical and pessimistic about everything you do. Being around them often drains your energy.

○ They put very little effort into the relationship, but expect you to go the extra mile for them.

They're controlling:

○ They have an image of who you should be, and when you don't measure up to that image, they make you feel terrible about yourself.

○ You often need to become someone else in order to make them happy. If you feel you can't be your true authentic self around someone, that's a real red flag.

○ They rarely let you express your feelings and often make you feel you're overreacting or doing too much when you're simply being yourself.

THREE SIGNS OF HEALTHY RELATIONSHIPS THAT WILL BUILD YOUR CONFIDENCE

They support your independence:

○ People who give you space to live life on your own terms are keepers. They understand that sometimes you will need to prioritise your personal needs over theirs and that's OK.

○ They don't make you feel bad about setting boundaries and don't take your independence as a sign that you don't love or need them.

They support your potential:

○ They use their words to build you up instead of tear you down. They are your biggest cheerleaders, they encourage you to go after your goals and help you see positive traits in your life that you don't even see in yourself.

○ They give you space to flourish and are inspired by your success instead of feeling jealous of it.

They support your needs:

○ They know your love language and they love you the way you want to be loved, not the way that's most convenient for them.

○ They give you space to communicate your needs and actively create an environment where you feel loved and protected. They listen when you speak.

Once you've identified the signs, you've got to learn to set boundaries with the confidence killers and get intentional about building your support system. To do that, you've got to invest in the relationships around you. Contrary to popular belief, relationships take work. Not work in the sense that it's laborious, but work in the sense that it requires intentionality. For example, I schedule in friendship dates and calls the same way I schedule in work meetings. I send certain friends funny memes to let them know I'm thinking of them even when I can't have a full-on conversation. I ask my close friends what their love languages are, so I know what makes them feel special vs what makes them feel left out. You've got to schedule in time to really connect with people, be present and actually listen, so they know they matter to you and that you hear them.

Humans don't form strong bonds over perfection, we form bonds over authenticity and vulnerability, so don't just talk about how amazing your life is, be honest and open up about some of your troubles to people you trust and share what you're learning from the challenging experiences. There's a clear line between 'misery loves company' and bonding over a shared experience. If your conversations are only ever about what's going wrong, how you're a victim or not good enough or you're seeking sympathy, then that's not authentic vulnerability.

Finally, being a positive, supportive and encouraging person goes a long way. People might forget what you've said but they'll never forget how you made them feel. Actively supporting someone's dreams is magnetic, as is showing up for them and bringing positive energy, and it's very likely they'll reciprocate in turn.

Going back to the golden rule: confidence isn't perfection. However confident you are, you will still experience fear, setbacks, self-doubt and all the other crazy bits of this rollercoaster we call life. But if you give up when it gets tough, you lose the battle against fear. Who wants to do that? And what if your challenges aren't there to break you, but to help you grow?

Having a creator mindset and focusing on what we *can* control are essential steps to bouncing back from setbacks. And let's not forget how crucial it is to create a safe haven of people we can rely on for support and ask for help when we need it. True authentic friendships with genuine love and support are a gift like no other. I know #selfloveisthebestlove is thrown around constantly in our #girlboss #independentwoman society, but feeling a sense of belonging and that we are loved is arguably just as important and something we should all prioritise a bit more. It's not to say our worth is determined by our relationships and we should become obsessed with receiving love from others. We are all already whole and complete, and our relationships are simply an added bonus that goes a long way.

If you struggle to build genuine connections with people, use some of the practical tips I've shared in this chapter. Also, take personal responsibility for whatever healing you need to do to open yourself up to love and friendship again.

Bouncing back from setbacks isn't easy, so if you're reading this now, congratulations, you've survived 100 per cent of the challenges that have come your way, and now we're going to look at how you can begin to succeed on your own terms.

7

KILLING IT! SUCCESS ON YOUR OWN TERMS

When you think of success, what's the first thing that comes to mind? Money? Fame? Followers? Titles? Power?

For the longest time, success for me was all about numbers. From my obsession with how much I weighed and what grades I got as a teenager to the number of likes and followers I had as I started to build my public profile as a confidence coach. The more likes and followers I had, the more successful I felt.

Now in theory, this view of success made sense, because when I looked at all the people the world called 'successful', they were wealthy and had power and influence, so naturally I strived for the same thing. After a while, though, I started to notice that this 'success' never felt satisfying enough. Once I had 5,000 followers, I wanted 10,000. Once I had 10,000, I wanted 30,000. Success that focuses on numbers never leaves you feeling satisfied, because there is always the possibility of more. You can end up feeling as though you're on a never-ending hamster wheel.

Another downside of this view of success is that it feeds off comparison, because there will always be someone with a better number than you. Regardless of your goal, there will always be someone with more money, more fame, more responsibility, a more successful business or a bigger family than you currently have. That's just life. We're all at different points on our journey through it, and the moment we define our success in relation to what someone else has achieved, it completely diminishes all our efforts. So, 10,000 followers looked like absolutely nothing when I looked at someone my age who had one million followers. For the longest time, it seemed that other people controlled whether I was deemed successful or not. I never felt that I could own it myself. Can you relate?

I'm not going to lie and say success isn't important to me. It is. I want to be successful, and it's not a crime to want that. A lot of us want to be successful. But success doesn't always have to mean money, power and fame.

A woman who is Confident and Killing It must learn to define success on her own terms. She must learn to rely less on the world for validation and make her own choices that bring her deep fulfilment.

#CAKIMantra

A confident woman must learn to operate from a place of wellness, purpose and passion and not define herself by her material possessions, financial position or a culture that is actively working against her liberation. In this part of your journey, you'll learn not to let the world's superficial definitions of success rob you of the deep pride and acceptance you should feel for yourself, you'll learn what a healthy and empowering version of 'Killing It' could look like and you'll get the opportunity to create your own. The final element of the PERMA five pillars of wellbeing model is 'A' for 'Accomplishment'. Psychologists have concluded that to 'achieve wellbeing and happiness, we must look back on our lives with a sense of accomplishment: "I did it, and I did it well."[1] Creating and working toward goals helps us look forward and build hope for the future. People who look back at their lives with a sense of accomplishment feel more optimistic and confident about their future because they know if they did it before, they can do it again. It's a huge source of motivation. Seeing, feeling

A WOMAN WHO IS **CONFIDENT** AND **KILLING IT** MUST LEARN TO DEFINE SUCCESS ON HER OWN TERMS. SHE MUST **LEARN** TO RELY LESS ON THE WORLD FOR VALIDATION AND **MAKE HER OWN CHOICES** THAT BRING HER DEEP FULFILMENT.

#CAKIMantra

So, if your definitions of success and failure make you feel insecure... change them.

and acknowledging your success makes you more confident, and when you're confident, you're more likely to share your skills with others and even inspire them to achieve their own goals. This is why it's so important to experience some level of success in your life. Even if you might not be where you want to be yet, or even if there are so many people ahead of you, everyone is worthy of success. So, if your definitions of success and failure make you feel insecure... change them.

Let's look at what happens when you follow the world's definitions. Success on anyone else's terms but yours will leave you feeling inferior to others and exhausted by the effort to keep up.

Remember that comparison feels a lot like driving a car and looking everywhere but ahead of you? Stop reading for a second and just continuously turn your head from left to right and see how it makes you feel. You're dizzy, it's hard to focus and you can't think straight, right? When you're busy looking at what other people are doing and never focusing on your own lane, it's a car crash waiting to happen.

When your pursuit of success feels like endless striving that's robbing you of your joy, then you know something is wrong. I'm sure you've all heard the saying 'Comparison is the thief of joy', but have you ever thought about how it does that?

We know we shouldn't compare ourselves to other people, yet we still do it. That happens because a lot of the time we aren't even aware of it. It's one of those things we do on autopilot. So, if we have any real chance of tackling this thief, we need to become more aware of its tactics and create our own comeback for it.

STOP COMPARISON STEALING YOUR JOY

In Chapter 2, you learned how to reframe negative thoughts and turn limiting beliefs into more empowering ones. That's exactly what we're going to do with comparison. We're going to question the lies, ditch them and create a new truth.

WHEN COMPARISON SAYS...

'LOOK AT HOW TERRIBLE YOU ARE AND HOW PERFECT THEY ARE...'

You can challenge it by saying, 'No one is perfect, and I embrace the beauty in my strengths and struggles.'

Say it out loud.

Why is this true? It's true because you never know what's going on behind the scenes. For the majority of the time, what people show you online and in person is a curated version of themselves. It's simply a highlights reel and not the full picture. So, comparing the worst of yourself to the best of someone else isn't even a fair comparison.

Getting really personal here, this particular lie was the biggest driver of my negative thoughts as a teenager. The Mean Girl in my mind would say, 'Look how flabby your tummy is and how skinny your sister is... Look how chunky your legs are and how long her legs are.' Back then I didn't have the awareness I have now, so I sat in that misery, feeling that my sister had it all and I had nothing. Only to later find out that when she saw me, she saw someone who was intelligent, outgoing and confident (no focus on my body whatsoever).

I was able to turn this comparison on its head by beginning to focus on my purpose and the things I loved about myself. Realising that I, Tiwalola, was bigger than my insecurities was a life-changing moment for me.

Your insecurities are a part of you, they aren't the whole you.

#CAKIMantra

Get curious about all the things you are capable of rather than dwelling on all the things you're lacking. There is beauty in your strengths and your struggles. We tend to know our struggles all too well and forget that there are strengths to be explored and acknowledged. Get practical by making a list of all the things you love or appreciate about yourself and reflect on them regularly. Reread Chapter 4 and remind yourself of the power of ditching perfection and embracing vulnerability. Comparison pushes you to have unrealistic expectations of yourself and when you don't reach them you feel unworthy. When you set goals, check in with a coach or accountability partner that they are realistic.

WHEN COMPARISON SAYS,

'LOOK HOW SUCCESSFUL THEY ARE, THEY'RE WAY AHEAD AND YOU'RE SO BEHIND...'

You can challenge it by saying, 'Someone winning doesn't mean I am losing. I am grateful for where I am while I'm on the way to where I'm going.'

Say it out loud.

Why is this true? It's true because the beauty in life is really in the process, not at the finish line. There are 7 billion or so people on Earth – there's no way we can all be at the exact same point in our journeys. Some will be ahead of us and some will be behind, but what really matters is that we're better than who we were yesterday.

CONFIDENT AND KILLING IT

YOUR INSECURITIES ARE A PART OF YOU, THEY AREN'T THE WHOLE YOU.

#CAKIMantra

So remember, it's not you against the world. Your biggest fear shouldn't be that someone else is better than you. Your biggest fear should be that you had the opportunity to grow and evolve, but never seized it. You stayed the same person your whole life, never daring to leave your comfort zone or bet on yourself.

Get practical by celebrating your big *and* small wins using the Confident and Killing It Monthly Wins Tracker. The MWT is a tool you can download for free at confidentandkillingit.com that encourages you to track your small and big wins every month with visibility of the whole year, so you can see your journey. This tool is powerful because whenever we feel we're not making progress, or comparison is getting the better of us (which happens a lot), we can remind ourselves of how far we've come. Slow progress is still progress and the late bloomer still blooms, so breathe and trust the divine timing of your life.

When you're consistent with sowing your seeds, what's yours will never miss you.

#CAKIMantra

The harvest is coming.

WHEN COMPARISON SAYS...

'THEY BEAT YOU TO IT, THEY'RE ALREADY DOING IT WELL, THEY'RE MORE POPULAR THAN YOU ARE, THERE'S NO POINT IN EVEN TRYING...'

You can challenge it by saying, 'No one has walked the same path as me. My story is unique and I'll own it. Plus, there's enough room for all of us to thrive.'

Say it out loud.

Why is this true? Because we all have a secret sauce. No one has lived the same life as we have, so we have unique views, perspectives and nuances. Take Rihanna, for example. She started her make-up brand Fenty Beauty in 2017. At the time, household names like Estée Lauder, Elizabeth Arden, Chanel and L'Oréal had been around for up to one hundred years and had dominated the market. Did the world really need yet another make-up brand? Probably not, but did Rihanna see an opportunity to add her own unique perspective as a Black woman to the beauty industry? Yes! So she went ahead and four years later the brand was valued at $2.8 billion. Did you hear that? *Billion*, with an annual revenue of $5 billion in 2021. Imagine if she'd never started. Imagine if she had said, 'There are already so many make-up brands out there, I don't have anything special to offer.' So that idea you've had on the back burner because you think there's no room for you, sis, I'm here to tell you to start now!

One of the things I love most about having a growth mindset is believing that there is enough room for everyone to be successful. If you operate in spaces where no one wants to give you a seat at the table, build your own!

CONFIDENT AND KILLING IT

WHEN YOU'RE CONSISTENT WITH SOWING YOUR SEEDS, WHAT'S YOURS WILL NEVER MISS YOU.

#CAKIMantra

Abadesi Osunade, a friend and mentor who has played a pivotal role in my entrepreneurship journey, really embodies this mindset. She was tired of the micro-aggressions and sidelining she was getting from being a Black woman in the UK tech industry, so she left her job to start her own company and community called Hustle Crew, which is all about delivering effective training and workshops that make tech companies more inclusive.[2] She used her personal experience to build her own table and she's absolutely thriving!

If you're not up for starting your own thing, you can always look for companies or environments that value your insight and experience.

Get practical by writing down key moments in your life that have shaped you and why. This will remind you of moments that have made you the unique individual you are today. And if you want to launch something but you're afraid that no one will care, speak to your potential customers, find out what their needs are, where the gaps are and then build together with them.

WHEN COMPARISON SAYS...

'EVERYTHING COMES SO EASILY TO THEM, LOOK HOW HARD YOU HAVE TO WORK AND STRUGGLE...'

You can challenge it by saying, 'I don't know what opportunities, knowledge and support they've had, so instead I'm going to focus on investing in my growth, my creativity and my confidence.'

Say it out loud.

Why is this a fact? Because unless you're God, you actually have no idea how much or little work someone has put in behind the scenes to get to where they are now. So, before you compare your Day 1 to someone who has been in the game ten years longer than you, or before you forget about someone's privilege and only look at their fancy opportunities, take a moment and focus on your own goals. You never know what someone has been through to get where they are, but what you do know is that you have the power to invest in yourself and become the woman of *your* dreams.

Get practical by listening to podcasts and interviews, reading books and hearing the full story of people you admire and the journey they've been on.

If life still looks easy for them, find out about the behind-the-scenes systems, processes, habits and possible privileges that have benefited them. And remember: 'Someone winning doesn't mean I am losing. I am grateful for where I am while I'm on the way to where I'm going.'

WHEN COMPARISON SAYS...

'IF YOU DON'T GET THE SAME THINGS THAT EVERYONE ELSE HAS, THEY WILL JUDGE YOU OR EXCLUDE YOU FROM THE GROUP...'

You can challenge it by saying, 'My goal isn't to be liked by everyone, my goal is to be my true authentic self.'

Say it out loud.

Why is this a fact? The truth is, if people really like you for who you are, they won't care about what material things you have or don't have. Clout chasers only care about what being friends with you gives them access to – this isn't real friendship. So if friends cut you off because you can't afford the same lifestyle they all have and they don't want anyone messing up their appearances, then be very grateful to be out of such a toxic environment. Any relationship built on material things won't last. Please know there are people out there who will love you for who you are. Life isn't the *Mean Girls* movie. If you can't be your true authentic self around your friends, then hunny, you need new friends. No one wins when people fall in love with a fake version of you.

Get practical by reflecting on your values and the things that really matter to you. Plus use the tips from Chapter 6 about relationships (*see p.249-251*) to take stock of the people in your life who are really in your corner. At the end of the day, people won't remember you for what you looked or dressed like, but they'll remember you for how you made them feel, they'll remember you for your character and the impact you had on those around you. Material things are fleeting, so get deep and really prioritise things that bring you long-term fulfilment.

RECAP: DAILY MANTRAS TO STOP COMPARISON FROM STEALING YOUR JOY

○   'No one is perfect, and I embrace the beauty in my strengths and struggles.'

○   'Someone winning doesn't mean I am losing. I am grateful for where I am while I'm on the way to where I'm going.'

○   'I don't know what opportunities, knowledge and support they've had, so instead I'm going to focus on investing in my growth, my creativity and my confidence.'

○   'My goal isn't to be liked by everyone, my goal is to be my true authentic self.'

○   'If they are winning, I can win too. Their success is a sign that it is possible for me too.'

○   'There is enough room for everyone to thrive.'

○   'If opportunities can go to them, opportunities can come to me too.'

○   'No one has walked the same path as me. My story is unique, I just have to own it.'

○   'Everything I need to win in life is already within me. I just need to wake up to it.'

○   'I will not doubt my greatness and I will not be scared of my potential.'

- ○ 'My success isn't defined by numbers.'
- ○ 'I can trust the divine timing of my life. My best days are still ahead!'

The only time comparison makes sense is when you use it as fuel to motivate you to be better. For example, if your friend can get over her social anxiety, then you can too. If that person on social media can be disciplined enough to prioritise their health, then you can too. If your comparison sounds like 'If they can do it, I can do it too' then it's healthy. Checking in on what other people are doing can give you creative ideas, help you read the room and give you a feel for what's going on in the world. It can even give you a vague idea of what to expect on your own journey.

When in doubt, always ask yourself if a thought feels empowering or sabotaging and remember the **#CAKIMantra**:

If it sabotages you, *bin it.*
If it empowers you, *run with it.*

#CAKIMantra

HOW TO REDEFINE SUCCESS ON YOUR OWN TERMS

Now that you have the tools to navigate comparison, it's time to break the rigid box of expectation surrounding what success looks like.

The moment I realised I was defining success all wrong was when I came across this Maya Angelou quote:

> *'Success is liking who you are, liking what you do, and liking how you do it.'*

So powerful yet so simple. Nothing about numbers, nothing about popularity, nothing about wealth. It put my success back into my own hands and made it feel achievable. I might not be able to control how many followers I got or how quickly my business grew, but I could fully control choosing to like myself and my work and valuing my progress. That's what motivated me to create my Monthly Wins Tracker. I began to see that success wasn't a destination I'd ever arrive at but was something that I could achieve at every stage in my life.

It also got me thinking about how real success was about honouring your values rather than ticking society's boxes. Is it success if you're making money but hate every moment of your job? Is it success if you have to constantly sacrifice your health to reach your goals? I'll leave you to answer that.

Now I know this is easier said than done, and the Nigerian in me is asking if self-love is going to pay my bills? But I wouldn't share anything with you that I personally haven't seen results from. For example, my first opportunity to work with one of the world's biggest companies, in my first year as an entrepreneur, came from this new way of thinking.

It was June 2020 and I had started running my own confidence masterclasses when all my corporate sessions got cancelled. Tickets were £20 and my goal (what success looked like to me) was getting at least ten people into a class. One weekend only two people signed up, and I'm not going to lie, I was disappointed and embarrassed. My Mean Girl kicked in. 'You should cancel this workshop. This doesn't look good and people are going to think no one rates you.'

I was on the verge of freaking out when I heard Maya Angelou's voice ringing in my head: 'Success isn't about numbers, it's about liking who you are, what you do and how you do it.' She was my ally in that moment. I paused and reframed my thoughts. In that moment, success was no longer about how many people came to the workshop, but about whether I was brave enough to honour my purpose and run the session in the first place. Designing the content, promoting it and showing up on the day was really all the success I needed. I decided to go ahead and run the workshop with just two people, and I was

'Success is liking who you are, liking what you do, and liking how you do it.' — Maya Angelou

determined to run it as if my life depended on it. Because there were only two people, it felt like a very bespoke, VIP experience, and the participants were excited to get me all to themselves.

Remember the **#CAKIMantra**:

Confidence isn't an absence of fear, confidence is feeling the fear but doing it anyway.

#CAKIMantra

I didn't let my fear of looking like a failure stop me from taking action, and in doing that, I added one more point to my confidence meter.

At the end of the session, I found out one of the women worked at Google and she loved the session so much that she went back and told her whole team about me and they booked me in for two workshops in October. Those two sessions have now led to over six employee engagement workshops at Google and they are my second biggest client. Imagine if I'd cancelled the workshop? Imagine if I'd moved the women into a bigger group later on? Would the stars have aligned like that? Who knows! But what I know for sure is that running away from failure didn't guarantee me success. I experienced true success when I focused on impact over numbers and made my own rules. I continue to do that.

The 'Killing It' in Confident and Killing It is less about capital gain and more about self-actualisation. It's not about being a boss and climbing to the top of a ladder or going to extreme lengths to progress 'at all costs'.

Last year I tweeted my definition of Confident Girl Summer, which went like:

Confident girl summer is a season of being unapologetic in your glow, being where the money resides, embracing the body you have, laughing more, living more, owning your greatness and killing it all day, every day.

Ninety-nine per cent of people loved it but then someone asked, 'Do I have to kill it all day, every day? That sounds exhausting.' In her mind, 'Killing It' probably looked like non-stop hustle, perfection and trying to have it all at the same time, and yes, that would totally be exhausting. I don't want that for any of you. If the idea of growing and evolving feels stressful, then you're probably in the wrong lane. For me, killing it every day looks like living in alignment with my Power Circle, where my strengths, passions and values meet. It looks like creating a life I'm proud of. The idea of doing what excites me rather than what drains me.

I can't tell you exactly how you should define success, because at the end of the day it's quite personal and there isn't only one way for a woman to be successful. However, since finding a definition that helped me feel more autonomous and patient with myself as I navigated life, I've done some more research and curated a list of three elements that can help you form your own healthy definition of success.

Here are some perspectives to consider when it comes to defining success on your own terms:

CHOOSE IMPACT AND QUALITY OVER POPULARITY AND QUANTITY

Success isn't about how much money you make. It's about the difference you make in people's lives.

— *Michelle Obama*

It's about changing lives, even one life, not about how many bums you get on seats or sales you make. It's about the quality of your relationships with people, not about the number of people you know.

PRIORITISE YOUR VALUES OVER SOCIETY'S EXPECTATIONS

To live the lives we truly want and deserve, and not just the lives we settle for, we need a Third Metric, a third measure of success that goes beyond the two metrics of money and power, and consists of four pillars: wellbeing, wisdom, wonder, and giving.

— *Arianna Huffington*

Success is no accident. It is hard work, perseverance, learning, studying, sacrifice and most of all, love of what you are doing or learning to do.

— Pelé

The media's portrayal of women over thirty and our society's obsession with looking young forever have really created a lot of unnecessary fear. Forget the list of things you need to do by the time you're thirty. Fulfilment comes from knowing what matters to you and doing just that. Questions like: 'What brings me meaning and joy?' 'What helps me rest and recharge?' 'What work or activities make me feel alive?' 'What do I value most in life?' will help you identify your values so you can prioritise them.

What I see when looking at the lives of the women I know over thirty is that your twenties are definitely not your prime. They're more like your primer. Many women have described their thirties to me as their 'no bullshit' years. By then they care less about what other people think, they're better at setting boundaries, they feel more secure in themselves *and* they have more wisdom, more experience and make more money. Sounds like the dream. So remember that 'Killing It' doesn't have to be about getting to the top of your game or ticking all the boxes before you turn thirty. It can also look like inner peace, consistent happiness and really doing whatever makes you feel fulfilled whether the world gets it or not. Turning thirty isn't the end for you – in fact, there's a lot more life to be lived – and no one has the right to make you feel a failure for not ticking all the boxes.

Here's a list of thirty things you *don't* need to have by the time you're thirty:

1. A marriage.

2. A house.

3. Kids.

4. Clear skin.

5. A degree.

6. A perfect credit score.

7. Your dream job.

8. Your dream body.

9. Your own business.

10. A side hustle.

11. Another language.

12. Designer items.

13. A solid friendship group.

14. Thousands of social media followers.

15. A six-figure income.

16. Cleared all your debts.

17. Reached your full potential.

18. Found your purpose.

19. Been made a director or executive.

20. Gone on your dream holiday.

21. Completed your bucket list.

22. Been intimate.

23. Solo travelled.

24. Bought a car.

25. Run a marathon.

26. Gone on a date.

27. Moved out of your parents' house.

28. Finished university.

29. Done a masters.

30. Become known in your industry.

CHOOSE CONSISTENT GROWTH OVER ONE-HIT WONDERS

Dreams are lovely. But they are just dreams. Fleeting, ephemeral. Pretty. But dreams do not come true just because you dream them. It's hard work that makes things happen. It's hard work that creates change.

— *Shonda Rhimes*

Hard work beats talent when talent doesn't work. Everyday wins build up to powerful, transformational change. Don't miss out on those small miracles because you're fixated on one big magical moment.

Success is about so much more than money and fame, and there's no one way to be successful.

The same thing applies to when you're 'manifesting' success. Some people think this is just about thinking positive thoughts, saying, 'I want, I want, I want,' and then sitting back and waiting for the universe to deliver a big moment of success. That's not quite how it works. Manifesting success is about intention followed by action and then faith. You believe in positive possibilities, you believe you deserve good things and that your dreams are possible and then every day you do something to take you one step closer to that dream and at the same time you don't obsess over the how and when of it happening. You don't obsess over the timeline and the exact outcomes. You set the intention, show up, play your part, trust the process and then have faith that it will all work out for you.

For example, let's say you're manifesting getting a promotion at work. Obsessing over a specific timeline in which to achieve this might end up in you feeling disappointed or putting so much pressure on yourself that you lose sight of your values because all you care about is reaching the finish line. Instead, take the necessary steps: do your job well, communicate your value, go the extra mile and then have faith and patience that the opportunity for promotion will come at the right time.

Nature does not hurry, yet everything is accomplished.

— *Lao Tzu*

When you're consistent with sowing your seeds, whatever is meant for you won't miss you, so don't be in such a hurry for a big break that you begin to despise the baby steps and ignore the small wins and mini miracles happening for you every day. See success as a mindset you can create for yourself here and now. It comes in many forms and there are multiple areas of your life where you can have different levels of success.

I hope this chapter inspires you to ditch mindless striving and instead opt for prioritising your wellbeing and fulfilment and knowing yourself well enough to do what works for you. Success is about so much more than money and fame, and there's no one way to be successful. A stay-at-home mum can be 'Killing It', a recent grad can be 'Killing It', the CEO of a Fortune 500 company can be 'Killing It'.

In the next chapter we'll look at how we *own* our success, because even after most of us have stopped obsessing over numbers, we still struggle to acknowledge our greatness. Why? There are a whole host of barriers holding us back. But before we deep dive into those, let's wrap up this chapter by remembering some key truths. If your definition of success makes you feel exhausted, stressed or a failure, change it. Your life, your rules, your pace – you can define success in a way that works for you, because you are worthy of being and feeling successful. Don't wait for someone to validate you and don't compare your wins to someone else's, because comparison will steal your joy. Protect it instead by focusing on your lane, being proud of the person you're becoming and honouring the gifts and passions within you.

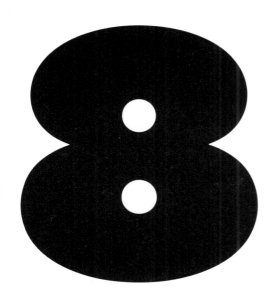

EMBRACING YOUR MAIN CHARACTER ENERGY

Welcome to my favourite chapter, where you'll learn how to show up and speak up confidently in all areas of your life. In case you don't know, you are *that girl*! You're an icon, you're a legend, you're the whole table plus the snacks. If you want to stop playing the supporting role in someone else's life and step into being the main character in your own life then we're about to make that happen.

In the previous chapter you defined success in your own way; now it's time to fully embrace it. Let me start by saying there is no award for playing small just so other people don't feel bad about themselves. You're doing a disservice to yourself and to the world. Being a confident woman doesn't mean being the loudest in the room either and this is certainly not a guide to being arrogant. Embracing your main character energy is about creating your purpose and owning your voice, your accomplishments and your personal story. You'll learn how to communicate your purpose and value, whether in your career or in your relationships, so you can create an aura that exudes confidence and a personal brand that attracts opportunities.

Articulating your value and then learning how to communicate it with confidence are so important, because you can be the most skilled and talented person in the world, but if you struggle to project a sense of certainty in your abilities or to articulate what you need in your relationships, people will tend to overlook you.

Every time I've run a workshop, I've received nothing but glowing feedback about my energy and the level of confidence I exude. This is something I've learned to do and you can too. Let's get into it!

CLARIFYING YOUR PURPOSE

When we embrace main character energy we're not just getting loud for the sake of it, we're getting loud because there is meaning and purpose to our life that can make the world a better place when amplified the right way.

As you learned in Chapter 1, purpose is something you can create for yourself. You don't have to wait for someone to give it to you or validate your existence. Your purpose is whatever you choose. All I suggest is that you make sure it's in alignment with your strengths, passions and values.

We're going to look now at creating a purpose statement. You can use the following questions to help you come up with keywords. Similar to passion, purpose isn't static, so don't worry about getting this 100 per cent right. You can always tweak it as you grow and evolve.

QUESTION	YOUR RESPONSE
1. What would you love to get paid for? (Think of work that energises you.)	
2. What skills/strengths/craft do you use to accomplish your answer to Q1?	
3. By doing what you love, whose lives do you want to impact and why? *(Think of a specific person/group and the problems they face.)*	
4. How will they change as a result of you doing your answer to Q1? *(List tangible and emotional changes.)*	
5. Why does this matter?	

Now you've done a bit of a brainstorm, you can get a bit more concise with your answers and put them into single, straightforward and punchy sentences. Again, there's no right or wrong answer and there's no pressure to have this all figured out right now.

LEVEL-UP:

CREATE YOUR PURPOSE STATEMENT

1. I am here to..._____

_____

_____

_____

_____

_____

_____

2. I do this by..._____

_____

_____

_____

_____

_____

_____

3. I am here to help..._____

_____

_____

_____

_____

_____

4. As a result of my work they experience..._____

_____

_____

_____

_____

_____

5. This matters to me because..._____

_____

_____

_____

_____

_____

_____

_____

Now that you have a clearer idea of why you're here, what you can offer, who you want to serve and the impact you can make, you can now move on to the next section, which is about communicating this purpose with confidence!

OWNING YOUR VOICE

The second part of embracing your main character energy is about owning your voice. Regardless of where you are on your journey, being a confident communicator is essential.

GETTING SASSY WITH NEGATIVE THOUGHTS

A lot of people struggle to speak up because of the negative thoughts they have about what will happen when they do. These often sound like:

- 'What if I say something wrong or stupid?'

- 'Everyone here is smarter than me, my opinion really doesn't matter.'

- 'What if people judge me or laugh at what I've said?'

- 'What if my partner calls me unreasonable when I express myself?'

- 'What if my friends think I'm doing too much?'

Ever said any of those to yourself? Yup, we've all been there. Time to challenge those negative thoughts using the Negative Thought Detector from Chapter 2.

Let's take 'What if I say something wrong or stupid?' as an example.

QUESTION 1:

'IS THIS 100 PER CENT FACT OR AM I MAKING AN ASSUMPTION?'

If you can think, 'What if I say something wrong?', you also have the option of thinking of the positive possibility: 'What if I say something right?'

QUESTION 2:

'WOULD I EVER SAY THIS TO A FRIEND?'

Think of the advice you would give a friend who was nervous about sharing one of her ideas and then give that advice to yourself. Be your own cheerleader.

QUESTION 3:

'DOES THIS THOUGHT SABOTAGE ME OR EMPOWER ME?'

Telling yourself you're going to say something wrong or stupid stops you from speaking up. In this case a more empowering thought could be: 'My opinions matter and I deserve to share my ideas. If I say something wrong, I am only human and I'll learn from my mistakes.'

Your mind is a battlefield of conflicting thoughts. Your negative thoughts are likely to be your default, but it doesn't have to be that way. If you have a fear of public speaking or speaking up in meetings, write a list of all the negative thoughts that come to mind when it's time to speak up and take each one of them through the Negative Thought Detector. Ditch the ones holding you back and create empowering thoughts you can believe instead.

THE 3VS OF COMMUNICATION

Once you've overcome any mindset barriers to communicating confidently, you can then move on to the physical elements of showing up confidently.

The 3Vs are the three most important elements to think of when it comes to being an impactful communicator. They are visual, vocal and verbal communication.

1. *Visual communication* looks at your posture, body language, dressing and gestures. The first thing people notice is your appearance. Make sure you're dressed appropriately for the occasion and that you're comfortable. Your posture should always be upright and your body language should be open and energetic instead of closed off and sluggish. Practise doing the Superman pose by placing your hands on your hips with your legs apart, and take deep breaths to feel secure and grounded before you speak.

2. ***Vocal communication*** involves your tone of voice and the pace at which you speak. The top speakers in the world are excellent storytellers. They know how to create anticipation, they know when to speed things up and slooooooow them down so they can land their point. Most importantly, they speak with *conviction*. They speak as though they truly believe in every. single. word. they are saying.

   My number one rule for public speaking is to only speak about things you really know and care about. Passion is important if you want to captivate your audience.

   Also, if you're giving a presentation and/or speaking in public, don't do the whole thing in one tone of voice. That will be way too monotonous and people will switch off. When you want to get your audience excited by an idea, speak more quickly with more energy. When you want people to feel the impact and weight of a point, then slow down with calmer energy.

   Another thing is to not be afraid of the silence. Silence can be a powerful tool in helping your message sink in. Silence doesn't have to be awkward.

3. ***Verbal communication*** is about the content of what you're actually saying. If you want to be a confident communicator, you need to know your stuff. Do your research, practise and use language that your audience will understand and relate to. Fancy words don't make you look smarter. Let your message be accessible.

HOW TO CONFIDENTLY HAVE DIFFICULT CONVERSATIONS

It's one thing to be a confident communicator when everything is going according to plan, but what happens when things get a bit challenging?

Here are five steps you can take:

1. **Have the conversation**
    Avoiding tough conversations in order not to upset people can cause you to harbour resentment and unforgiveness which seriously outweighs the benefits of staying quiet and keeping the peace. Also, our meaning-making machine of a brain will start making assumptions, trying to mind read the situation which makes things look worse off than they actually are. Apply everything you learnt in Chapter 5 about overcoming fear and just do it!

2. **Be open and listen**
    Once you've brought up the issue, be open and listen to what the other person has to say in response. Don't just listen to respond with a script you've already created in your head. Really listen to understand their point of view and reasoning.

3. **Use 'I' statements**
    The moment you start pointing fingers at someone they'll get defensive and on edge. When their guard is up, communication shuts down and nobody wins.

Using statements like 'from my perspective...'
'I felt this way when you did this...' 'This is what
I understood from what was said...' will keep the
conversation focused on your experience, thoughts,
feelings and reactions and not on judgements you've
made about the other person. For example 'I felt
intimidated by your response' has quite a different
impact to 'you were cold and aggressive towards me'.

4. **Be solutions orientated**

Before you start a difficult conversation, have a few
ideas of how the situation can be resolved or positive
changes that can be made so the other person can
see you are committed in finding a way forward and
not instigating conflict for no reason.

5. **Follow up after some time**

Always check in a few days or weeks later with
the person you've had the difficult conversation
with. Sometimes people need a bit more time to
process information so following up and checking
in makes sure the person knows that they matter
and are heard.

And if you're on the receiving end of a difficult
conversation, try not to internalise it by thinking
someone is calling you a bad person. Good people
can make mistakes. Be open and listen, take on the
lessons you've learnt and commit to doing better
next time.

CAN INTROVERTS BE CONFIDENT COMMUNICATORS?

Confident communication isn't just reserved for the extroverts in society. Whether you're an introvert or extrovert or a bit of both, you can learn to communicate with confidence. Again, this isn't just about being the loudest in the room, it's about showing up with an energy that says:

✦ I know who I am.

✦ I trust in my abilities.

✦ I deserve to be here.

Introverted readers, I'd love to encourage you to take the fundamentals of the 3Vs and apply them in your life in a way that works for you. Introversion isn't about a lack of confidence but actually just a characteristic of those who get energy from internal thought and solitude vs those who get energy from large social interaction and attention (extroverts). In fact, many of us have both introvert and extrovert tendencies, it's rarely either/or. Rosa Parks, Gandhi and Bill Gates are introverts who have led amazing big-scale missions that have impacted society in a positive way.

The goal here is to understand your personality traits and use them to your advantage. For example, according to Susan Cain, author of *Quiet Power*, introverts tend to make amazing leaders and entrepreneurs, because they are creative thinkers, good listeners and not obsessed with power. In a negotiation, being a good listener means you can pick up on cues other people tend to miss and, as an entrepreneur, it allows you to fully understand the needs of your customers so you can confidently create solutions to meet those needs, and in relationships, it allows your partner to know they are heard and seen, which builds trust and an environment for you to show up as your true authentic self.

If you look at the ingredients of powerful communication – looking the part, speaking with authority, conviction and passion, knowing your stuff and listening intently – they can all be accessed by both introverts and extroverts.

If you've noticed, on social media we have the Confidence Queens who are loud, fiery and make you want to jump up and take action immediately when you hear them speak, and we also have the Confidence Queens with soft, soothing voices who make you think deeper and feel at peace within yourself in a way that inspires you to make better choices (personally, I feel I'm somewhere in between). The groups have very different communication styles and yet are equally impactful.

Whether it's in meetings or at home you can find a communication style that works for you and own your voice. No more apologising for asking a question or apologising for your appearance on Zoom. No more padding your requests with buffers like 'no worries if not' or self-deprecating talk like 'This might sound silly but...' or 'I'm not sure if this will make sense...' or 'It was so stupid of me to do that' one hundred times a day. If you know the answer, then own it and say it straight up. If you don't know the answer, then own it too and go and look for a solution.

OWNING YOUR SUCCESS

In Chapter 7 I introduced the Monthly Wins Tracker to help you acknowledge your successes, but from time to time you've got to go one step further and actually *talk* about them. Yes, that's right, getting comfortable with self-promotion and openly talking about your successes is a vital part of building confidence and the third part of embracing your main character energy.

I know as soon as I said 'self-promotion' some of you already started feeling cringed out by the idea, but in all honesty, 'self-promotion' isn't a bad word. Being Confident and Killing It is about questioning and challenging rules and beliefs in society that might be holding you back. Well, self-promotion and being arrogant or boastful are things I've challenged and reframed over the years, and you might just want to do the same.

To me, self-promotion is simply an exchange of value and enthusiasm, whereby you have something to offer the world and someone out there needs what you have, and so you get

Get strategic about showcasing your expertise and building a reputation, so the people looking for what you have can find you.

strategic about showcasing your expertise and building a reputation, so the people looking for what you have can find you. Self-promotion is, in itself, a neutral act; it's just a form of self-expression. The responsibility for doing it the right way lies with the individual and their intentions. Shallow people promote themselves in shallow ways. Authentic people promote themselves in impactful ways. If you have integrity and depth, you're likely to promote yourself in an authentic way, a way that also aligns with your values.

I know there is an argument for moving in silence, not sharing your dreams with everyone and not letting your left hand know what your right hand is doing, because not everyone wants to see you win and the haters are real. However, we can learn to be selective in what we share and how we share it, so we don't completely cancel out all the benefits of self-promotion.

One of my London-based clients, Yvonne Bajela, came to me because she wanted to get better at self-promotion and owning her accomplishments. The idea was so alien to her that she didn't even post on social media when she made it to the Forbes 30 under 30 list (yeah, I know!) Whenever she talked about self-promotion, I could see her body get tense and by her facial expressions and the sound of her voice, I could tell she was sooo put off by the idea. It simply went against everything she believed in.

To get her to open up to the idea, I first had to identify her core values. You'll remember your values are your main drivers for motivation, so if you want to start a new habit or change the way you think about something, see how it aligns with your values.

After using the Values exercise in Chapter 1, we identified Yvonne's core values as being action oriented, purpose driven and a thought leader who's a wealth of knowledge for start up founders. Next up, we identified how self-promotion could help her honour and live out her values.

Here's what we came up with:

VALUE	HOW SELF-PROMOTION CAN HELP YVONNE HONOUR HER VALUES
Being action oriented.	Talking about her successes could help her reflect and remember the positive actions she took to get there, which could then help her challenge imposter syndrome and self-doubt when experiencing challenges in the future. She'll remember if she did it before, she can do it again, and so she'll be motivated to keep working hard and taking action.
Being purpose driven.	If purpose is being of service to something bigger than yourself and doing impactful work, then self-promotion could help amplify her message and meaningful work which could lead to even more impact at scale. Potential funders seeking investment could hear about her story or a recent win and give her opportunities that would allow her to continue doing impactful work and living her purpose.

<table>
<tr><td>Being a thought leader and wealth of knowledge.</td><td>Yvonne didn't make the 30 under 30 list for nothing. She made it because she was clearly an expert in her field. Now there are young founders who need her expertise and who can learn from her experiences, but how will they do that if she doesn't talk about her journey, her lessons and her wins? How can she honour her value of being a wealth of knowledge for people if she doesn't share that knowledge?</td></tr>
</table>

After a couple of sessions, Yvonne started sharing more about her wins and life lessons online and at work and it led to more paid speaking engagements, interviews and overall fulfilment for her, as well as making her knowledge and insights more accessible for the people she wanted to help the most. It was a win-win.

So, as you can see, self-promotion doesn't have to be used in a boastful or arrogant way. It's a great way to own your success and show the world the value you can offer, so you can continue to attract more opportunities to live out your purpose.

CONFIDENCE CHECK-IN: CREATING MEANINGFUL GOALS

The technique that I used with Yvonne, of aligning your goals with your values, can be used in other areas of your life where you need motivation to start a new habit or even a business. Feel free to create your own version of the table on the previous page. For example, pick something in your life you've been putting off and write down how doing that activity can help you honour the values you identified in Chapter 1.

MYTHS AND TRUTHS ABOUT SELF-PROMOTION

Here are some myths and truths about self-promotion to help you reframe it in a way that can be used to build your confidence:

Myth: **It's arrogant, it's superficial, it makes you look full of yourself.**

Truth: **There's a difference between confidence and arrogance...**

Arrogant people only think of themselves. They want to be at the top and push everyone else below them. They have an 'I'm better than you' mentality and they shout about their accomplishments in a very self-centred way.

Confident people, on the other hand, know that they are amazing, but they think about how they can use their gifts to lift others up. They understand there's enough room at the top for everyone and they have an 'I'm amazing, but you're also amazing too' mentality. When confident people self-promote and talk about their accomplishments, they focus mostly on the lessons they've learned and how those lessons can be used to help and inspire other people.

Myth: **Promoting yourself makes other people feel bad about themselves.**

Truth: **When you do it in the right way, people tend to be more inspired by your success than demoralised by it.**

This is why aspirational marketing is so powerful. Behavioural scientists have also studied the power of role models in getting young people to follow a positive trajectory in life, and research shows that if people of a similar background to you see you win, it opens up their minds to believe it's also possible for them.[1] Because if you can do it, they can do it too.

When you have confidence, you'll think, 'I'm really proud of myself for doing this. Let me share some lessons I've learned that could help other people too.' This is aimed at lifting others as you climb.

If you celebrate yourself in an authentic and inclusive way and people still feel a certain way about it, you've got to make peace with the fact that at the end of the day, you are not responsible

IF MY **LIGHT**
IS TOO BRIGHT
FOR YOU,

GO AND
PUT SOME
SUNGLASSES
ON.

#CAKIMantra

for other people's emotions. If someone feels insecure about themselves after seeing you succeed, that's a choice they've made and they need to sit and ask themselves why you winning is triggering them in a negative way. As I always say:

If my light is too bright for you, go and put some sunglasses on.

#CAKIMantra

You're not here to please and fix people. You're here to live the one life you have to the fullest! If they don't like you or your energy, they can leave the room! But no more shrinking.

In my podcast episode with Sofi aka The Oddity, a fellow Confidence Queen, vlogger and all-round good vibes, she said, 'Instead of dimming your light to sit in darkness with another woman and make her feel more comfortable in her insecurity, why don't you give her an extra light bulb so you can both shine together?' How powerful is that? Nobody wins when you dim your light. You are way too worthy and valuable to sit on the sidelines. You are the main character. Own it.

Research shows that if people of a similar background to you see you win, it opens up their minds to believe it's also possible for them.

Myth: **I just need to put my head down and let my work do the talking.**

Truth: **Your work will not speak for itself *alone*.**

Society has sold women the lie that we need to keep our heads down and let our work speak for itself, but data shows that 21 per cent of women get passed over for promotion compared to their male counterparts, so something isn't adding up![2] Interestingly, when 240 senior leaders of a Silicon Valley tech company were asked to name the factors that got them promoted to their level, making their achievements visible was named the most important factor in their advancement![3]

There is no award for being the world's best kept secret.

#CAKIMantra

You are way too worthy and valuable to sit on the sidelines. You are the main character. Own it.

CONFIDENT AND KILLING IT

THERE IS NO AWARD FOR BEING THE WORLD'S BEST KEPT SECRET.

#CAKIMantra

Imagine if Nike decided not to have a marketing budget and just let the products 'speak for themselves', they wouldn't be the number one sports brand in the world. They make quality products, but they also have incredibly large marketing budgets to tell stories and create moving media and content around the products that entice you to buy and join the Nike community.

Hiding your gifts isn't the same thing as being humble. You can be humble and believe you are good enough to succeed. You can be humble and celebrate yourself for how far you've come. A lot of people use being humble as an excuse not to own their accomplishments, but really there's a couple of things hiding behind that humble mumble. One of them is imposter syndrome, you downplay your achievements because you're afraid that if people dig into your success, they'll find out that you're not that good and you don't really know what you're doing. You never want to look like too much of an expert, because if someone asks you a question you don't have an answer to, or gives you a piece of work that's too challenging, you'll be seen as a failure. When you play small there's less risk of judgement and shame, so you stay in your comfort zone, saying you're humble when really, you're hiding from your greatness. Another thing that hides behind being humble is a fear of judgement; this one isn't actually that surprising, as studies show that women who self-promote and speak authoritatively sometimes experience backlash for failing to show stereotypical 'feminine

You can be humble and celebrate yourself for how far you've come.

traits' (such as being humble, nurturing, and collaborative).[4] It's a double-edged sword: engage in self-promotion and run the risk of being criticised for being boastful or arrogant, or fail to self-promote and limit your growth by getting side-lined and not taken seriously. Can we ever win? I like to believe we can. Is the backlash fair? No. But we can't wait for gender bias to be eliminated before we live life to the fullest. So what can we do? Focus on what we can control and use the resources available to us. The tools I've shared in this chapter can help you work around the hurdles you might encounter for being a woman who is confident and unapologetic in owning her accomplishments. Here are few more to consider:

○ Host a Lunch & Learn session at work to showcase your knowledge, skills, passion and accomplishments in a certain area.

○ Create a culture or habit of celebration by starting or ending meetings or gatherings with each individual sharing a recent win – I personally do this with my team.

○ Put together a report of best practices, lessons learnt and team accomplishments after you've wrapped up a project and cascade it to senior management, clients or share as a case study.

○ Be a cheerleader for others and encourage them to celebrate their wins when you see them happen.

On a whole, sharing your success with the lessons you've learnt and best practices for others to implement ensures you're lifting others as you climb. If you still get labelled as arrogant or aggressive when you're unapologetic in communicating your value and speaking up for yourself, escalate the situation to HR for further support and consider whether the environment is worth staying in. Protect your sanity and choose your battles.

OWNING YOUR PERSONAL STORY

Every main character has a storyline. If you're going to truly step into your main character energy, then you're going to need to create and own your personal story. In a world where everyone has an opinion of who you are and what you are capable of doing, owning your narrative is a powerful form of resistance.

In the *School of Greatness* podcast, Lewis Howes described a personal brand as the 'digitisation of your reputation'. It is your ability to show and communicate the results you have achieved at scale. If you are achieving excellent results but no one knows about it, you don't have a strong personal brand or a reputation for delivering value. Scale doesn't need to be a million people. This isn't about being famous, it's about making sure the right people, however many they are, know who you are, what you can do and what you stand for, because at the end of the day if you're living out your purpose and being in the service of something bigger than yourself, you can't achieve it all on your own.

Our human-to-human connection is a strong driving force behind why and how we make decisions. Studies show we are more likely to buy from or give opportunities to people we trust and have an emotional connection with.[5] A personal brand is important here because it allows you to build connection, trust and excitement with people in a very organic way.

In 2020, a Statista report showed 85 per cent of the UK population used the internet to find information about goods and services before they purchased.[6] If you're a freelancer or entrepreneur, you could really lose out on potential business if you don't have a strong digital presence. That said, don't feel like a failure if you don't have one; everyone's journey is unique and some businesses might not require a strong digital presence as such. If the set up you have is working for you then keep doing it!

A personal brand also isn't just for entrepreneurs or influencers. If you're on the career ladder, having a reputation at work for delivering value increases your visibility and chances of getting a promotion. Having positive connections with people could mean you get chosen more often for new opportunities, you have people championing you because of the value you have brought them and you might even be able to get insights from others that could help you do your job better. According to a 2018 CareerBuilder survey, 70 per cent of employers use social media to screen candidates during the hiring process.[6] In a competitive job market with a sea of overqualified candidates, having a personal brand is a huge asset.

Everyone has a reputation for *something*. Building a personal brand is just a smart way to get strategic about owning your narrative. In 2017, for example, no one really knew who I was.

Building a personal brand is just a smart way to get strategic about owning your narrative.

By 2021 my name had become synonymous with confidence building for women. As you can see, that didn't happen overnight, but it did happen intentionally. For the first two years of running my business full time, I didn't need to send a single outbound email looking for work, because literally all my opportunities kept coming to me. In fact, the deal that led to this very book you're reading came from having a strong personal brand. I got about four different emails from publishers, saying, 'I've seen your Instagram and listened to your podcast and I love what you stand for, have you ever thought of writing a book?' My opportunities to work with Google, UN Women, *The Sunday Times*, Morgan Stanley, Oatly, Glamour, Meta (Facebook), Warner Music and Snapchat all came from having a strong reputation (i.e. results at scale) as someone who delivered impactful and innovative confidence workshops.

How did all of these opportunities come my way? Well through a combination of hard work, self-promotion, a strong personal brand and referrals from other people. Creating and owning your narrative allows you to amplify your purpose because stories travel, stories connect with people. When you hear a good story, you share it. Embracing your main character energy by owning your personal story opens many doors for you to impact the world in a positive way and inspire others to do the same.

BUILD YOUR PERSONAL BRAND

Instead of just letting the world put labels on you, here are three practical steps you can take to build a strong personal brand that feels authentic and organic and establishes trust with your audience, colleagues, potential prospects and anyone else you come into contact with.

Step 1: Identify your USP (unique selling point)

Here are five questions to help you articulate who you are, what you love and what you stand for:

1. What problem do you or a certain group of people face that you really want to solve or have already solved?

   For me, it was the generational cycle of low self-esteem in women and girls. How about you? What's something that makes you so upset you really want to do something about it? Remember the prompts from the level-up exercise in Chapter 1: what do you talk about, cry about and dream about?

2. What do you want to be known for? What characteristics do you want people to associate you with?

I'd recommend aligning your personal brand goals with your Power Circle – your top strengths, passions and values – so your brand is authentic in terms of who you are now. Of course you can always have new areas for growth, but your brand shouldn't feel inauthentic.

3. What sort of projects have you completed and what was it about your specific input that made those projects successful?

4. What sort of projects and tasks do people tend to approach you with and trust you to handle?

5. What industry(ies), field(s), occupation(s) or business(es) do you actually want to be in? How do you ideally want to spend your time?

Look for patterns in your answers to these questions. Once you've identified some, get intentional about building on them.

Quick caveat: We live in the era of multi-hyphenates and don't have to be known for only one thing! I'm known for confidence, but I'm also known for travel, podcasting, dancing, business and financial empowerment. I suggest picking a core theme and start there. You can add more later. I believe we all have the choice of full creative expression and we don't have to box ourselves up, but at the same time being associated with a million different things dilutes your personal brand. So keep themes complementary rather than random.

For example, if you took a glimpse into my life through what I show and talk about on social media and in person, you'll see my core theme is confidence and my complementary themes are travel and lifestyle, financial empowerment and entrepreneurship.

Another example is Jackie Aina. Judging from how we've seen her show up online, her core theme is make-up, hair and championing diversity and inclusion in the beauty industry, and her complementary themes are luxury fashion and lifestyle, self-care and general life hacks.

Step 2: Communicate your USP

Once you've nailed your themes, it's time to start letting the outside world know about them. There is no limit to personal branding. It can go beyond the digital world. As we've seen, the aim of a personal brand is to help people build a connection with you, and this can be done both online via social media and personal communications, and offline via meetings, networking events, fairs, courses and workshops, and one-to-one conversations. In this section, we're going to look at content and conversation prompts to help you speak about yourself and your brand in a way that connects with people on a deep level.

YOUR STAND	LIFE STORIES	LIFESTYLE
Social controversy	Meet the founder	Behind the scenes
Industry challenge	The wins/ strengths	Interest one e.g. beauty
This matters to me...	The losses/ failures	Interest two e.g. travel
Quotes I connect with	Lessons learnt	Interest three e.g. food

THOUGHT LEADERSHIP	RESULTS	QUESTIONS TO YOUR AUDIENCE
Business related topic one	Case studies	Who they are
Business related topic two	Media mentions	Interests & aspirations
Business related topic three	Partnerships/ collaborations	What are their behaviours
Business related topic four	Testimonials	What are their struggles

YOUR STAND	It's important to show people what you stand for and embody the values you believe in. This is also a great way to start a conversation with your audience, teams, clients and those around you. Talk about an industry challenge or a hot controversial topic that's relevant to you. Share your thoughts on things that matter to you.
LIFE STORIES	No one has been on the same journey as you. Your story is unique, and sharing it allows people to connect with you. Before sharing, ask yourself, 'What's the value in this?' Share your wins, but also share your mistakes. Focus on the lessons you've learned. Only share a challenging story once you have processed the experience and healed from it. If you feel that your story owns you, then it's not the right time to share it.

LIFESTYLE	This is a chance to introduce light-hearted content or conversation and notice who in your environment has the same interests as you. This is also where complementary themes come into play. Humans are multifaceted, so don't be afraid to show other sides of yourself if you feel comfortable with doing so. This is completely optional. Some people never show parts of their private life on social media or at work and that's totally OK. Do what works for you.
THOUGHT LEADERSHIP	This is where you show your expertise and knowledge, so people can build confidence in who you are and trust what you say. Write blogs and how-to guides and share your opinions and comments alongside other people's work. When you're in meetings, speak up and share your thoughts and ideas. Your voice matters, so use it!

RESULTS	Sharing positive results is important. This isn't boasting or showing off. When people know more about what you do and see you deliver results, more opportunities come your way. If you work in a team, find a balance between taking personal ownership for your success and giving credit to your team when it's due. As we've seen already, owning your success is also a great way to improve your confidence.
QUESTIONS TO YOUR AUDIENCE	Keeping in touch with your audience, colleagues or clients is crucial to building a real connection. Get to know them so you can continuously offer value. Check in with people, understand what challenges they are facing and work with them to find solutions.

These pointers will help you take your personal brand from a concept to something you live out day to day. Use your style and uniqueness to attract the jobs, clientèle and friends that you want.

Step 3: Identify key channels and be consistent

Pick a few content and conversation prompts from the previous table to use on your chosen online and offline channels. When building your digital presence, you will burn out if you are creating new content on every single social media platform. Instead, do some research on which platforms best suit your goals, lifestyle and audience's habits, then be consistent with it. For example, if you prefer to express yourself through visual mediums, Instagram, Pinterest, YouTube, TikTok and Facebook are best suited for your needs. And if you prefer to express yourself through the written word, platforms like Medium, Reddit, Twitter and LinkedIn may work better for you. There's no one-size-fits-all approach when it comes to choosing the right platform to share on, but one golden rule is to repurpose content where you can and use tools to help you manage the planning and scheduling.

Building a personal brand takes time and effort, but it's worth it. And the need for a personal brand will continue to rise. The steps we've just covered are an easy and accessible way for you to get started, so if you haven't taken it seriously in the past, now is the best time to start.

So, as we wrap up this section, remember every main character has a voice and owns their story. Communicating your worth, celebrating your accomplishments and owning your personal story allow you to be confident as your true authentic self, unapologetic about who you are and what you have to offer.

As we learned in the PERMA model for optimum wellness, research from positive psychologists shows that people who look back at their life with a sense of accomplishment feel more optimistic and confident about their future. Celebrating yourself by owning your successes isn't arrogant, it's an essential pillar of your wellbeing. In this life you *have* to be your own cheerleader, because there will be people out there who don't believe in you or your dreams, and they will seize every attempt to humble you and put you in your place. There will be people who will try to limit you and your potential. But never forget that your opinion of yourself matters more than what other people think of you. Learn to believe in yourself even when others don't, and don't wait for anyone to validate you or give you permission to live your life. You're the main character. It's your life, your pace, your rules. As we've seen, part of being Confident and Killing It is deciding which 'rules' in society serve you and which don't, and then letting go of what's holding you back so you can continue to evolve into the fullest and most beautiful version

Your opinion of yourself matters more than what other people think of you.

of your authentic self. You only get one chance at life, so learn to see the beauty in owning your purpose, your voice, your successes and your personal story.

In the next chapter we're continuing with the main character energy by learning how to prioritise ourselves. Our needs, our wants, our dreams, and anything else that matters to you! But for now, learn to fall in love with your story and embrace the fact that no matter how big or small your achievements, you are always worthy of sharing your voice and celebrating your success. Life is a gift, and a precious one we shouldn't take for granted. Our presence alone is a present to the world.

Remember, you are 'Killing It' in your own right. You're an icon, you're a legend and you are the moment.

9

PRIORITISING YOUR NEEDS

Every time you're given a choice between disappointing someone else and disappointing yourself, your duty is to disappoint that someone else. Your job throughout your entire life is to disappoint as many people as it takes to avoid disappointing yourself.

— *Glennon Doyle*

As we come to the end of this journey we're going to look into how we create long-term wellbeing instead of the yo-yo self-care journey that most of us are on – work super hard, burnout super hard, rest for a bit then do it all over again. Life doesn't actually have to be that way. A fancy holiday is no substitute for making structural changes to live and work in a more sustainable way. You can achieve your goals *and* be confident, wealthy and well rested. (I really like the sound of that: #wealthyandwellrested.) Would you work on developing a growth mindset, believing in your capabilities, overcoming fear and embracing your main character energy just to throw it all away because some people don't like how you've started prioritising yourself? Absolutely not.

There is honestly nothing worse than spending your whole life living for other people instead of prioritising your needs and living the kind of life you *really* want to live. Your worth is not tied to your ability to please others or to achieve goals. Your worth is intrinsic and nothing can take it away. In *What a Time to Be Alone*, Chidera Eggerue says 'For the world, I'll always be too much of one thing or not enough of another, but for myself I will always be enough.'

In the previous chapter you articulated your purpose statement; by this point you might be feeling super energised and ready to take on the world. You may even be doing this as we speak, but holddddd on, we're in this for the long run. We're here for a good time *and* a long time, so in this final part of the book I'm going to challenge you, but in the most loving way so you can get better at protecting your peace and energy.

The Glennon Doyle quote that opens this chapter has inspired me a lot because, to be honest, nobody has died from being disappointed, so if you have to set boundaries, prioritise your growth and choose yourself. *Do it*, because at the end of the day, people will be alright. Never sacrifice your health just to achieve a goal, because if you die, *who will do the work?*

I can speak from experience, because in 2020 I experienced burnout. I didn't realise you could burn out doing work you were passionate about, so I was in denial about it for the longest time. It wasn't until I literally felt as if my soul had left my body and I had nothing else to give that I realised how real it was.

Burnout is described as 'a total loss of energy and interest and an inability to function effectively, experienced as a result of excessive demands on one's resources or chronic overwork'. It looks like:

○ An inability to control your emotions or feeling no emotion at all. Out-of-control emotions often reflect the out-of-control demands we put on ourselves. On the other hand, some people might experience a serious lack of motivation, joy and fulfilment. You feel empty, like you have nothing left to give.

○ Feeling overwhelmed by daily activities that would usually be a breeze. It's like the weight of the world is on your shoulders and you're paralysed by all the decisions you need to make.

○ A lack of self-care – you skip showers, hardly eat or overeat, work constantly and lose touch with your body and what it needs.

○ Irritation – you start resenting people for no real reason and feel disconnected from the people you love most. You dread being around people and get irritated easily.

○ In severe cases, it manifests itself as physical symptoms like headaches, body pain, difficulty sleeping, anxiety and tightness in your chest.

DITCHING THE PEOPLE-PLEASER IN YOU

One of the reasons I was suffering from burnout was due to the people-pleaser in me. I'm such a 'yes' person, I have real Superwoman syndrome. As we learned earlier, the Superhuman is one of the five imposter syndrome personas created by Dr Valerie Young. Superhumans are the people who say 'yes' to everyone and everything because they've tied their worth to their ability to help others. In friendships, this can look like helping a friend through a break-up when you don't have the emotional bandwidth to really listen and support. At work, this can look like saying 'yes' to a project with a ridiculously tight deadline because you want to look good in front of your boss. If you're a freelancer, it looks like saying 'yes' to every opportunity that comes your way because you're not sure when the next one will come.

Society has conditioned us to believe that saying 'no' makes us unreliable and a fraud, even selfish, while saying 'yes' and pleasing people makes us reliable and capable. It also makes us feel needed and wanted. These are all very important and valid emotions, but we must learn to access them in a way that isn't detrimental to our health.

The key word here is 'balance'.

It is possible to please others without neglecting your own physical and emotional needs.

#CAKIMantra

IT IS POSSIBLE
TO PLEASE
OTHERS
WITHOUT
NEGLECTING YOUR
OWN PHYSICAL
AND
EMOTIONAL
NEEDS.

#CAKIMantra

There's a reason why on planes they ask you to put your own oxygen mask on *before* helping others. No matter how skilled and strong you are, you have a personal limit. If you take on too much, you will break. You are not a rock, you are human, and humans are delicate.

So, when I talk about prioritising your needs, I'm not saying be individualistic, egoistic and self-obsessed. What I'm saying is you should fill up your cup first then give from your overflow. You'll be a better giver when your batteries are charged. Nobody wins when you go through life as a burnt-out version of yourself instead of the glowing and thriving woman you deserve to be.

If you take on more than you can handle, you are also literally opening the door to imposter syndrome, because as soon as you mess up or drop the ball, your Mean Girl is going to charge in with: *'I told you so* – you don't have what it takes to do this job!' or 'You see, you're a bad friend and no one is going to like you anymore.' But you're not suffering from imposter syndrome because you're incapable of doing your job, but because you've overstretched yourself and are right in the stress zone.

I could have saved myself a trip to that zone if I'd been better at saying 'no' earlier on. Now that I know better and can easily spot my people-pleasing behaviour, I'm trying my best to make better decisions. Before you can do that, you've got to be aware of how people-pleasing shows up in your life. So let's get into that...

You're a people-pleaser if:

o You care a lot about how you look and what other people think of you.

o You find it hard to set boundaries with people and give more than you take.

o You prioritise everyone else's needs without thinking of how it will affect you personally.

o You always work overtime to please your boss or colleagues.

o You give your all to your relationships but often end up alone and hurt.

o You avoid confrontation at all costs.

o You are often stuck doing things you don't want to do because you find it hard to say 'no'.

o You apologise for a lot of things you don't even need to apologise for.

o You dim your voice and your light to make other people feel more comfortable.

o You often resent people for not caring about you as much as you care about them.

If you resonate a lot with the traits I've just mentioned, don't be alarmed – being a people-pleaser comes from a very natural human desire to be loved and accepted. The issue arises when we go the extra mile for other people and do the bare minimum for ourselves. You are worthy of more than the bare minimum, so start acting like it!

Your ancestors didn't fight for the emancipation of women just for you to enter the world and be a doormat.

Aside from burnout and imposter syndrome, another danger of being too nice is that you're probably attracting the wrong kind of people into your life. People who tend to neglect themselves in order to please others often attract users. I hate to break it to you, but they're not always asking you for help because they like you or you're the best person for the job, they're asking you because you're the person most likely to say 'yes'.

Your ancestors didn't fight for the emancipation of women just for you to enter the world and be a doormat. It's time to wake up and stop being so nice. Not a single woman has achieved something significant by being the nice, good girl who always did what she was told. Yes, be kind to others, be loving and caring, but never hide your real feelings and opinions for the sake of being agreeable. You'll end up coming out as quite bland and struggle to build real connections with genuine people.

The next time you want to hand out yeses like the time Oprah gave everyone in her audience a car: 'You get a yes, you get a yes, you get a yes…', stop and ask yourself this question: 'If I say "yes" to this, what am I saying "no" to as a result?'

For example:

✦ 'If I say "yes" to going out late the night before a deadline, I am saying "no" to peace of mind, rest and quality work.'

✦ 'If I say "yes" to that friend who is always asking for money, I am saying "no" to my own financial goals and progress.'

✦ 'If I say "yes" to that business opportunity that's paying too low, I am saying "no" to owning my value.'

If you keep saying 'yes' to everyone and everything while saying 'no' to yourself, your needs, your potential and your dreams, you will burn out, and I can tell you, burnout ain't cute! Let's learn to work smart and *rest*.

HOW TO REALLY REST

Rest isn't a 'nice to have'. It's not a luxury reward you get from overworking yourself. Rest is essential.

#CAKIMantra

No one has ever said, 'I'll eat once I've achieved my goals,' because food is essential fuel for the body and you most likely won't achieve anything on an empty stomach. I want you to view rest the same way.

Imagine you're about to set out on an eight-hour car journey and your fuel gauge is almost on zero. You're not going to say, 'Stopping for petrol is a waste of time – I'll just drive quickly and hope my car doesn't break down,' because you know very well that a car will 100 per cent stop working when there's no fuel left in it. Instead, you'd prioritise putting enough fuel in your car to do the long journey. So, why not prioritise resting and refuelling your body, mind and soul so you can achieve long-lasting wellness?

Rest isn't just about how many hours of sleep you get or a long weekend of Netflix and chill. According to Saundra Dalton-Smith, MD, author of *Sacred Rest: Recover Your Life, Renew Your Energy, Renew Your Sanity*, humans need physical, mental, social, emotional and spiritual rest. To avoid or bounce back from burnout, you need to make sure you're resting in the way that your body, mind and soul need at that moment.

PHYSICAL REST	
WHEN YOU NEED IT	**HOW TO DO IT**
When you feel exhausted, can't keep your eyes open or feel really stiff with body pains.	Get more sleep. Get a massage or a hot bath. Stretch your body, do some yoga or gentle exercise. Give your body grace. Moisturise your skin, then use a dry brush to get your blood flowing. Eat a healthy and wholesome meal.

EMOTIONAL REST	
WHEN YOU NEED IT	**HOW TO DO IT**
When your heart feels heavy and either your emotions are all over the place or you feel completely numb. You may be getting irritated easily and notice a consistent down mood.	Reconnect with your values and what matters to you most. Do something fun to spark joy. Acknowledge how you feel. Sit with your emotions for a bit and then process them either by journaling or speaking to someone you trust. Do some gratitude journaling. Write yourself a love letter. Get your nails and hair done. Tidy up your space and change your bedsheets. Start a new hobby. Reflect on your monthly wins using the Confident and Killing It Monthly Wins Tracker.

SOCIAL REST

WHEN YOU NEED IT	HOW TO DO IT
When you need time alone because your social batteries have been maxed out and, even as an extrovert, you're dreading seeing people. Alternatively, when you're feeling low and lacking a sense of community and connection and need to be around supportive people for a boost.	Check in with yourself regularly and slow down enough to listen to what your body needs. Whether you need some quiet time or time with great friends, schedule it in the diary. Here are some ideas: **Social rest with friends:** Sleepovers Boozy brunches Picnic dates Spa days Facetime **Social rest from friends:** Solo trips Long walks in nature Time with your phone off A social media cleanse Reading

MENTAL REST	
WHEN YOU NEED IT	**HOW TO DO IT**
When your brain feels foggy, you're struggling to concentrate, you're lacking creativity and you're heavy on the self-criticism.	Less screen time. More walks in nature. Mindfulness meditation. Gratitude journaling. Read a book. Listen to a podcast. Write out positive affirmations and stick them on your mirror.

SPIRITUAL REST	
WHEN YOU NEED IT	**HOW TO DO IT**
When you feel there's something missing in life or you've lost your sense of direction, purpose and inner wisdom.	Do something meaningful to help others, like volunteering. Put a smile on their face. Meditate and pray. Reconnect with your faith and listen to an inspiring message of hope. Make a vision board.

FINANCIAL REST

WHEN YOU NEED IT	HOW TO DO IT
When you're feeling stressed or anxious about money.	Check your money mindset, challenge your assumptions and ditch the sabotaging thoughts.
When it feels like you're drowning in debt.	Check the way you speak about yourself and to others when it comes to money. Ditch the shame and criticism for open honest conversation.
When you're scared about living from paycheck to paycheck with no emergency funds.	Review your statements regularly to understand how your money is being spent and look for small tweaks you can make for improvements. Remember baby steps lead to transformational change.
When your lack of financial stability makes you feel unworthy and full of shame.	Start building better money habits and get pro-active with your finances by creating different budgeting pots for holidays, eating out, shopping… and stick to them.
	Connect your money goals with your values so when you're saving, it's towards something meaningful.
	Use your ability to learn and level up to read up on investing opportunities to grow your money.

FINANCIAL REST

A lack of financial stability can cause us a lot of anxiety and stress that can affect our confidence and derail our goals so I felt it was important to add this in!

P.s. These are my personal tips for better financial wellness and should not be taken as legal financial advice.

Use these tables as a reference point you can go back to anytime you start to feel burnout creeping in.

I saw a quote on Twitter that said, 'If you don't pick a day to rest, your body will pick it for you,' and I screamed because we've actually all been there. Those moments when our body completely shuts down and goes, 'Nope, not today,' happen way too often in our generation, and frankly the level of stress we experience is not what our ancestors died for. When you're stressed you're more vulnerable to negative thoughts, low moods, procrastination and diverting from your goals. It's worth doing something about it when you feel life getting too much to cope with.

In his book *Think Like a Monk*, Jay Shetty describes one of the best morning routines I've come across, designed to cultivate peak performance, purpose and peace. His T.I.M.E. model has four steps to help you create time for yourself and prioritise your needs before everything in the world starts fighting for your attention:

✦ **T – Thankfulness.** Express gratitude every day. You can think it, sing it, write it or share it with a loved one. Gratitude is the foundation for a positive mindset and feels like a protective bubble shielding you from the negativity in the world. As I mentioned earlier, research shows that gratitude has a powerful effect on our psychological and physical health, so if you haven't started a gratitude journal yet, this is a sign to do it.

✦ **I – Insight.** Gain insight into something new by reading a book, listening to a podcast or a TED Talk. Starting your day by learning something new sets the tone for the rest of the day and cultivates a habit of being open to listen to, connect with and learn from others, which are traits of a good leader.

✦ **M – Meditation.** Meditation isn't just humming for hours with your eyes closed while secretly thinking of your next meal. A lot more creative expression can be involved. For example, spend 10–15 mins doing some deep breathing (I love the guided breathwork videos @breathpod and @yogitochi post on Instagram) or search for guided visualisations and 'I AM' affirmations on YouTube or on your podcast app. Try a few things and see what works for you, but essentially the goal is fifteen minutes of stillness every morning. Meditation helps calm the mind and cultivates focus. It also allows you to set your intentions for the day, instead of letting other people dictate how you show up. It is hard and your mind will wander from time to time, but just bring your attention back to your breath when it does. It's only when you get your mind still that you can really connect to the wisdom inside you.

 E – Exercise. This can be as intense or relaxing as you'd like; the goal here is just to get the body moving. Exercise boosts your energy levels and motivates you to take on the day. It's also a powerful way to combat stress and release any tension and negativity that's stored in your body.

When we start the day prioritising our needs and take T.I.M.E. every morning for ourselves, we set ourselves up for success. This is one of the smartest investments we can make in ourselves.

STOP FEELING GUILTY ABOUT RESTING

Knowing how to rest is the easy part; actually following through and overcoming the productivity guilt is where the next challenge lies.

I asked my community on Instagram, what came to mind when they thought of me, aside from confidence, 'enjoyment' was the most popular response. I was thrilled because I *love* enjoyment. I didn't come here to suffer #softlife. I'm here to live life to the fullest and that's that. The older I get, the more I realise how important it is to prioritise your happiness. I enjoy life loudly because I want other women to see that it's possible for them to also experience joy in their lives. There's no award for hustling to the point where your soul dies. I work hard, yes, I make shit happen, but I will prioritise enjoyment. So here are some reminders from your favourite minister of enjoyment about how to enjoy some guilt-free rest:

○ Self-care is a necessity. You need it, you deserve it and don't have to earn it through hard work.

○ Rest isn't the opposite of hard work, laziness is. Rest and laziness aren't the same. Rest enhances the quality of your life, laziness hinders your progress.

○ Your life is your responsibility. You are the author of your story, you write the rules of how your life plays out. You can allow yourself to rest.

○ There's no need to base your success or productivity on the toxic hustle culture that society has created, and that, btw, is not sustainable. Live life on your own terms.

If you feel guilty about putting your needs above those of others, I want you to remember that:

○ Prioritising yourself and your wellbeing doesn't mean disregarding those around you or being selfish. It's not about drastically cutting people off either. It's about making sure your oxygen mask is on before helping others. It's about filling your cup up first then giving from your overflow rather than from your minimum capacity.

○ Prioritising yourself is essential for your happiness. You will find yourself resentful and miserable when you continuously prioritise others over yourself, especially when that isn't ever reciprocated.

On the days when you're super busy and rest is the last thing on your mind, I want you to remember that:

○ You are at your most productive when you are energised and managing your emotions well, instead of feeling numb and drained. So, rest, then go again. Needing to rest is not a sign of defeat.

○ Don't wait to 'find' time to rest, 'create' the time. Put it in the diary. For example, I've blocked out time for #TiwaTime, gym sessions and dinner dates with friends in my diary because those are things I value a lot.

○ If this is something you really want to improve on, take a moment to articulate why wellness is important to you and how it takes you closer to the best version of yourself. Think about how it supports the goals and dreams you care about. Then actively make it a priority by using the technique you learned in Chapter 4 to align your to-do list or goals with your values for better work–life integration. That way your ambition won't come at the expense of your health.

Self-care is a necessity. You need it, you deserve it and don't have to earn it through hard work.

At the end of the day, learning to prioritise your needs is a mindset shift. If you feel guilty about rest, take a moment to redefine what rest means to you and look at how it can help you move forward in life.

Here are some affirmations to write multiple times in your journal or say out loud. Remember your mind is powerful and you can reprogram it to see rest in a positive light, rather than as something that hinders your success.

○ 'Even though life will be challenging, I deserve joy and fulfilment.'

○ 'I am important. My worth is not tied to my ability to please others.'

○ 'When I pour into myself, I can shine my light onto others.'

○ 'I am worthy of speaking my mind and having my needs met .'

○ 'I can make time to nourish my mind, body and spirit.'

○ 'Spending time on myself is always an investment and never a waste of time.'

SETTING BOUNDARIES AND PROTECTING YOUR ENERGY

Once you've overcome your mental blocks about prioritising your needs, it's time to take action by setting boundaries. Boundaries are simply a user manual for showing the people in your life who you are, what you want and how you want to be treated. Setting boundaries is about loving yourself enough to protect your wholeness and energy and being OK with disappointing others if it means not disappointing yourself. It sends a loud and clear message about the level of love and respect you feel you deserve.

With many things in life, even though we know we're meant to do them, we still kind of avoid them because of how hard they feel, so let's look at some simple ways to set boundaries.

ACKNOWLEDGE WHAT YOU GAIN BY SETTING BOUNDARIES

○ When you *set boundaries*, you say 'yes' to having your needs met and 'no' to feeling anger and resentment.

○ When you *set boundaries*, you say 'yes' to creating a feeling of physical and psychological peace and safety and 'no' to feeling disrespected and unsettled by certain people and places.

○ When you *set boundaries*, you say 'yes' to doing things that nourish and bring joy to your body, mind and soul and 'no' to things that drain your energy.

○ When you *set boundaries*, you say 'yes' to more confidence and security in who you are and 'no' to feeling unworthy.

○ When you *set boundaries*, you say 'yes' to more control over your life and 'no' to anxiety and stress, because you're no longer thrown into situations you don't want to be in.

○ When you *set boundaries*, you say 'yes' to attracting the right kind of people into your life and 'no' to people who manipulate you, flake on you, use you, make jokes about your insecurities and make you feel small.

So, in short, *set boundaries*.

PAY ATTENTION TO YOUR NEEDS AND DEFINE YOUR PRIORITIES

Really lean in now and feel your feelings. Remember not to care too much about what other people will think. Ask yourself important questions like:

○ 'Am I doing this because I really want to or because I feel pressured to?'

○ 'Do I really have the capacity to help a friend out now or am I afraid that they'll hate me if I say "no"?'

○ 'How do I feel after I've spent time with that person?'

When you set priorities, make sure you know your non-negotiables and the areas you're open to compromising on. This is where your values also come into play. Things that align with your values should be priorities, things that don't need to be let go of.

COMMUNICATE DIRECTLY, OFTEN AND BE ASSERTIVE

A lot of women fear being labelled as aggressive if they set boundaries and speak up, so they end up living very passive lives, letting people walk all over them. Let's put an end to that!

There's actually a clear difference between being aggressive and being assertive. Let's break it down:

THE PASSIVE PERSON	THE AGGRESSIVE PERSON	THE ASSERTIVE PERSON
Is afraid to speak up or speaks very quietly.	Continuously interrupts and loudly 'talks over' others.	Speaks openly in a conversational tone and knows when to speak and when to listen.
Shows little or no expression, usually avoids eye contact.	Often intimidates people with cold looks and body language.	Makes good eye contact and has warm and open energy and body language.
Isolates themselves from groups, usually in the corner.	Controls groups and wants everything to always go their way.	Participates in groups and is a good team player.

Avoids conflict and agrees with others, even if it goes against personal feelings, values and boundaries.	Usually causes conflict by only considering their own feelings and often makes selfish demands on others.	Doesn't instigate conflict, but remains confident and retains integrity in the midst of a disagreement.
Values themselves less than others and often neglects personal needs to please others.	Values themselves above others and always puts their personal needs first, while neglecting the impact on others; will often hurt others to avoid being hurt.	Considers themselves equal to others; knows when to prioritise their personal needs and when to compromise for others.
Doesn't reach goals and might not even have goals.	Reaches goals 'at any cost', usually at the expense of others.	Knows how to reach goals without hurting others or their own personal wellbeing.

Never be afraid of losing people by speaking your truth or stating your needs. It's your responsibility to tell people where your boundaries are, and if people stop being there for you because you've started prioritising your needs, then they never really cared for you in the first place.

How can you be both compassionate and assertive? This is what it sounds like:

- 'I'm sorry you're going through this, but honestly, I'm not in a good place to be there for you right now. Could we talk about it later?'

- 'I can't lend you any money. But is there another way I can help you out?'

- 'We don't seem to be agreeing on this, maybe it's best for us to just drop it.'

- 'Things have been so busy lately, I need to have some me-time. But shall I let you know when I'm feeling back on track?'

- 'I want to spend time with you, but I can't do that if we continue to talk about your ex/parents/politics, etc.'

- 'As much as I want you to be happy, I realise I'm not here to fix you or be responsible for your happiness.'

CONFIDENT AND KILLING IT

WHEN YOU DON'T SETTLE FOR THE BARE MINIMUM, YOU MAKE ROOM FOR BIGGER AND BETTER OPPORTUNITIES TO COME.

#CAKIMantra

START WITH SMALL ADJUSTMENTS AND BE CONSISTENT

Don't just dive straight into the deep end cancelling everyone who has crossed your boundaries. People make mistakes and so do you, so have some compassion! But do practise saying 'no' on a small scale, so you can get comfortable with it and more confident when it comes to making hard decisions in the future.

Also, pay attention to your mindset. Are you acting from a fixed mindset or growth mindset? A lot of people, including me, find it hard to say 'no' because you never know when the next opportunity will come. In 2020, I had no idea where my next month's money was coming from, so I said 'yes' to basically every opportunity that came my way, just in case the next month was a dull month and I made no money. But guess what? The opportunities never stopped coming, and before I knew it, I had more going on than I could handle. We live in an abundant world, so it's OK to be selective about your friends, relationships, career and work opportunities.

When you don't settle for the bare minimum, you make room for bigger and better opportunities to come.

#CAKIMantra

ESTABLISH YOUR BOUNDARIES IN A PROFESSIONAL SETTING

Any boss worth having knows that our job is an aspect of our life and not our whole life. Aside from our work, we have our home life, our relationships, our passions and our personal priorities to consider. But we spend so many hours of our life working that setting boundaries at work is essential to our overall wellbeing.

Whatever your work, some scenarios in which you'll need to be assertive and set boundaries are when:

○ A colleague keeps stealing your ideas and presenting them as their own.

○ You're continuously asked to work unreasonable hours or on tasks outside your remit.

○ You're being called into meetings unnecessarily and feel your time isn't being used properly.

○ A colleague's behaviour crosses your personal boundaries or values.

○ A colleague keeps trying to contact you out of office hours.

○ You're made to feel guilty about taking time off, rest days or sick leave.

Although it can be more daunting because of the power dynamics, setting boundaries at work is similar to setting boundaries in your personal life: understand and articulate what the problem is, know your non-negotiables, know what your preferred outcome is, and then confidently communicate those desires.

Here are some examples:

○ 'I've noticed you share my ideas without giving me credit. In future I would like you to reference me. Is that something you can do?'

○ 'I've noticed you send me emails and messages outside work hours. Moving forward, I'd prefer it if you could schedule your emails to be sent during working hours and then I'll endeavour to reply in a timely manner. Is that something you can do?'

○ 'In order to do my best work on this project, I can't take on any additional work right now. I'd be happy to check back in with you once my workload is lighter to see if you still need support. Does that work for you?'

When starting a conversation, remember not to let unnecessary apologies creep in. Saying things like 'Sorry to bother you, but I just wanted an update on this work' or 'I hate to be a pain, but could I please chat about my working hours?' or adding 'No worries if not' at the end of a request dilutes the effectiveness of your message and will make people less likely to take you seriously.

Boundaries are often broken because there are no clear expectations. Knowing what you want, how you want to work and communicating that regularly can foster healthier workplace relationships. It's important to mention that there will be some days when you have to work a bit later if you've got a tight deadline or situations where you have to pick up extra work as part of being a good team player. However, if you find that your boundaries are repeatedly disregarded, you might be working in a toxic environment that is beyond your control. In that case, it might be time to find a better environment that respects your personal and professional needs.

As we wrap things up, I want you to make a promise to yourself that from here on out you will regard yourself as highly as you regard those around you and prioritise your own needs.

Switching off often feels counterproductive but when you look at the bigger picture it sets you up for long-term wellness and success. You don't have to be a 'strong Black woman', you don't have to be a 'selfless mother'. You're allowed to be soft. You're allowed to rest. You can't dismantle the patriarchy and create a new world by being a slave to a non-stop capitalist culture.

As you go through life, discovering your authentic self, getting sassy with the Mean Girl, taking risks, embracing your main character energy and celebrating your success, remember none of this would be possible without a well-rested body, mind and soul. Prioritise yourself. Set boundaries. Being too nice invites people to come into your life, cause havoc and then leave you feeling empty and anxious. So, be assertive, ask for what you need and know that the people who really love and care for you want nothing more than to make sure you're living a rich and fulfilled life on your own terms. Make peace with the fact that you will outgrow some people and places. That's OK. When one door closes, another opens.

There is no one else like you in the world. You are one of a kind, a once-in-a-lifetime gem. Don't take your existence for granted. You deserve to be taken care of, pampered and loved. By yourself as well as by others.

You are a priority. Never forget that.

CONCLUSION

At the beginning of this book I asked if you had ever thought of what it would be like to have unshakeable confidence. Whatever your answer was, I hope that feeling feels a lot more achievable for you by this point. As we come to the end of this journey, my wish is that you are filled with hope. Not merely wishful thinking, but real hope that leads to determination, drive and a desire to give yourself the best possible life you can imagine. I know you are worthy of that, and now you do too, and that's the best part.

So what's next?

I can't promise that after reading this you'll never doubt yourself ever again, because you will. Confidence isn't the absence of self-doubt. It's about seeing the fear, the doubt and the imposter syndrome as signs that you must take action. Your greatest insecurities are often direct correlations to your greatest strengths, so when you feel that you don't deserve to be heard, speak up! Speaking up is exactly what you must do. When you feel you're not worthy of an opportunity, go for it! Pursuing it despite your feelings is exactly what you must do. When you feel you don't deserve rest, rest is exactly what you owe yourself. Before reading this book you may have been hiding your light, you may have been at the mercy of your Mean Girl or you may have been crippled by your past failures and rejections. From

When you feel you're not worthy of an opportunity, go for it!

this point on, these things no longer have power over you. You're not the same person you were when you started this book. You're awake now. And the awakened version of you has to start making better choices and creating new habits for the long run. Confidence is a practice, so if you think the job is done once you put down this book, well, think again. It's a never-ending journey and thankfully you'll always have this book as a guiding light through it all.

At its core this book is designed to equip you with the tools to thrive and flourish no matter what life throws at you. You now have the tools to identify and articulate your strengths, passions, values and purpose, which will make sure you are living a fulfilled life in alignment with your calling.

You can now get sassy with your negative thoughts and replace them with more empowering ones. So when things like comparison try to steal your joy, you can rise above it and change your perspective.

You now know that learning is your superpower, and knowledge and capability aren't the same thing, so when you're faced with something you've never done before, you'll be more inclined to bet on yourself, Learn and Level Up.

You now know that emotions aren't facts, they are just energy flowing through you and open for interpretation. Fear isn't the enemy. The worst possible outcome isn't the only possible outcome, so lean into the positive possibilities of your life. You also have the tools to define and celebrate your success in a way that works for you. No more romanticising over-achievement or dimming your light to make other people feel more comfortable.

Your mere existence is a gift to the world.

And finally you have the tools to set boundaries, prioritise your needs and identify the kind of rest that's right for your body, mind and soul.

My number one goal with this book was to get you to take positive action. What that would look like only you could say, but if you were feeling a bit stuck in a certain area of your life, you now have the tools, mindset and confidence to go forth and kill it. Get excited by the fact that every baby step is one step closer to your truest, most powerful self.

Confidence isn't a destination you arrive at overnight, so if you're still on the way, still processing things and need a bit more time to deal with feelings that have come up for you, take that time, and ask for help when you need it. It will be worth the effort.

And if one day you wake up and realise the things you value and desire have changed, that's OK too. It's a sign of growth and an opportunity for you to start this beautiful journey again, heading in a different direction. You can set out many times, learning and loving yourself over and over again until your very last days.

At the end of every coaching call, I give my clients the opportunity to make some commitments to themselves, a set of promises from this new place of enlightenment that they are going to honour. I want you to do the same.

What promises are you going to make to yourself?

There's enough room for all of us to be confident and thrive.

Confidence is about keeping the promises you make to yourself, so when you write down these promises, write them with conviction. Know why they are important to you and follow through on them. Don't make promises you think I'd want to see, or promises you think will impress the world: these promises are for *you*.

And if you don't always manage to keep them, nothing new there, your best will look different every day, just give yourself the compassion you so readily give to others and make sure you get back up again.

What you believe about yourself is the foundation to everything you do. Your opinion of yourself matters more than what anyone else thinks, so never let anyone place limitations on your life's expectations. It's better to be full of yourself than be full of other people's negative opinions that, frankly, do not matter! You are skilled, you have strengths and your potential is limitless!

And one of the beautiful things about being confident is that it's not something we have to compete for. There's enough room for all of us to be confident and thrive. So share the wisdom you've got from this book. Buy a copy for a woman or girl in your life. The next time you're in a room and it feels like the insecurity Olympics, be the person that changes the narrative, because no one wins when we are stuck in a vicious cycle of self-hate. Most importantly, be the change you want to see in the world.

I'd love you to share your Confident and Killing It moments #CAKIMoments with me online and keep tracking your wins in your Monthly Wins Tracker, to remind yourself you are absolutely good enough and to inspire other women who see you Killing It to believe they can do the same.

Join us in the Confident and Killing It Academy to access resources, live masterclasses and to connect with a buzzing community of bold women who will encourage you to shine your light. Life's way more fun when we're all Confident and Killing It *together*, so although this is the end of this book, it's the beginning of an exciting new chapter for us all.

ACKNOWLEDGEMENTS

My heart is filled with so much gratitude to every single individual that has played a part in the making of this book. First, I want to thank God for my gifts and for the strength to see this through to the end. Knowing that you are always faithful to your promises has been my anchor throughout this season.

To my family and friends, thank you for all the love and support you've given me from day one, I've never felt alone and for that I am truly grateful. In particular, I'd like to thank my parents Ade and Nike: I am who I am today because of you. Thank you for helping me see that there is no limit to what I can do and who I can become. Thank you for your constant prayers and working so hard to give me the best life and opportunities possible.

To my special person, my first love, Goke. Thank you for being my rock, thank you for being patient with me when my emotions were all over the place. I appreciate how much space you give me to shine and I've never met anyone who genuinely wants to see me succeed like you do. You're the best.

Ruth and Denique, my incredible team members. Thank you for your passion and dedication towards this mission. You made writing this book whilst running a business a better experience and you'll forever be a part of this story. To Nancy Adimora for being a guardian angel and sparking the idea for this book back in October 2020. Your words were a guiding light throughout the process.

Thank you Oscar Janson-Smith, my literary agent, for being an incredible ally and voice of encouragement on the days I doubted myself. It's been a privilege to have you in my corner. You've always gone the extra mile for me and for that I'm super grateful.

To my editor Zoë Berville, I honestly didn't know what to expect when I started this journey but working with you has been a dream. Thank you for pushing me in the most loving way, for the reassurance throughout and for really believing in me and my work. To the rest of the team at HQ and HarperCollins – Abi Le Marquand-Brown, Sian Baldwin, Becca Joyce, Stephanie Heathcote, Georgina Green, Harriet Williams, Ange Thomson, Darren Shoffren, Sara Eusebi and Halema Begum – thank you for the next-level hard work, dedication and enthusiasm you put in to make this happen behind the scenes. I'm so grateful to have been surrounded by such talented people.

And finally a very special thank you to my community, to everyone who has booked me to speak at their company, attended a workshop or event, signed up to the Academy, hired me as their coach, shared my videos, followed on social media, listened to the podcast and sent me messages of how much my work has helped you. On days when I felt like giving up your encouragement carried me to the end. I hope this book impacts your life as much as you have mine.

This is a win for all of us.

NOTES AND REFERENCES

INTRODUCTION

1. Chandler, Victoria, '61% of 10 to 17-year-old girls in the UK have low self-esteem according to new research', *Good Housekeeping* (5 October 2017). https://www. goodhousekeeping.com/uk/health/health-advice/a572286/ low-self-esteem-research-uk-teenage-girls/.

2. Kay, Katty and Shipman, Claire, 'The Confidence Gap', *The Atlantic* (May 2014). https://www.theatlantic.com/ magazine/archive/2014/05/the-confidence-gap/359815/.

3. Pofeldt, Elaine 'The Confidence Gap and Women Entrepreneurs', *Forbes* (28 May 2013). https://www.forbes. com/sites/elainepofeldt/2013/05/28/the-confidence-gap- and-women-entrepreneurs/.

CHAPTER 1: DISCOVERING YOUR AUTHENTIC SELF

1. Scott, Ellen, 'British Women Have the Second Lowest Self- Esteem in the World', *Metro*, 24 June 2016. https://metro. co.uk/2016/06/24/british-women-have-the-second-lowest- self-esteem-in-the-world-5964813/.

2. Winfrey, Oprah, 'What Oprah Knows For Sure About Finding Your Calling', Oprah. https://www.oprah.com/ spirit/oprah-on-finding-your-calling-what-i-know-for-sure.

CHAPTER 2: GETTING SASSY WITH THE MEAN GIRL IN YOUR MIND

1. 'Neuroplasticity', Psychology Today. https://www. psychologytoday.com/gb/basics/neuroplasticity.

2. 'About', Dr Jill Bolte Taylor. https://www.drjilltaylor.com/ about-dr-jill/.

3. Baikie, Karen A. and Wilhelm, K., 'Emotional and Physical Health Benefits of Expressive Writing', *Advances in Psychiatric Treatment*, 11 (2005). DOI:10.1192/ apt.11.5.338.

4. Phelan, Hayley, 'What's All This About Journaling?', *The New York Times* (25 October 2018). https://www.nytimes. com/2018/10/25/style/journaling-benefits.html.

5. 'Giving Thanks Can Make You Happier', *Harvard Health Publishing*, Harvard Medical School (14 August 2021). https://www.health.harvard.edu/healthbeat/ giving-thanks-can-make-you-happier#:~:text=In%20 positive%20psychology%20research%2C%20 gratitude,adversity%2C%20and%20build%20strong%20 relationships.

CHAPTER 4: DITCHING THE WEIGHT OF PERFECTIONISM AND PROCRASTINATION

1. Heath, Nicola, 'Are You a High Performer or an Over Achiever?', *INTHEBLACK*, CPA Australia (1 April 2021). https://www.intheblack.com/articles/2021/04/01/high-performer-or-overachiever.

2. OWN, 'Dr Brené Brown on Faking It, Perfectionism and Living Wholeheartedly | SuperSoul Sunday | OWN', (17 March 2013). https://www.youtube.com/watch?v=_YeuIUgWNp8.

3. 'Multitasking: Switching Costs', *American Psychological Association* (20 March 2006). https://www.apa.org/research/action/multitask.

CHAPTER 5: STARTING TO BET ON YOURSELF

1. Madeson, Melissa, 'Seligman's PERMA+ Model Explained: A Theory of Wellbeing', PositivePsychology.com (2 April 2022). https://positivepsychology.com/perma-model/.

2. Abrams, Abigail 'Yes, Impostor Syndrome Is Real. Here's How to Deal With It', *TIME* (20 June 2018). https://time.com/5312483/how-to-deal-with-impostor-syndrome/.

3. Coduras Martínez, Alicia et al., 'Global Entrepreneurship Monitor Special Report: A Global Perspective on Entrepreneurship Education and Training, 2010', Global Entrepreneurship Monitor (2010). http://entreprenorskapsforum.se/wp-content/uploads/2010/05/GEM-Special_report_entrepreneurship-training.pdf.

CHAPTER 6: LET YOUR BOUNCE BACK BE STRONGER THAN YOUR SETBACK

1. Levine, Irene S., 'The Seven-Year Expiration Date on Friendships', *Huffpost* (28 June 2009). https://www.huffpost.com/entry/the-seven-year-expiration_b_208468.

2. Moeller, Robert W. et al., 'Emotional Intelligence, Belongingness, and Mental Health in College Students', *Frontiers in Psychology*, 11 (2020). DOI:10.3389/fpsyg.2020.00093.

3. 'Relationships in the 21st Century: The Forgotten Foundation of Mental Health and Wellbeing', *Mental Health Foundation* (May 2016). https://www.mentalhealth.org.uk/sites/default/files/Relationships-in-21st-century-forgotten-foundation-mental-health-wellbeing-full-may-2016.pdf.

4. Maltz, Maxwell, *Psycho-Cybernetics* (Perigee Books, 2015).

CHAPTER 7: KILLING IT! SUCCESS ON YOUR OWN TERMS

1. Madeson, Melissa, 'Seligman's PERMA+ Model Explained: A Theory of Wellbeing', PositivePsychology.com (2 April 2022). https://positivepsychology.com/perma-model/

2. If you'd like the audio version, listen to Episode 34 of the *Confident and Killing It* podcast: https://podcasts.google. com/feed/aHR0cHM6Ly9hbmNob3IuZm0vcy8xZDdlM WY0MC9wb2RjYXN0L3Jzcw/episode/MDNjMWM0NjM tYTFiYS00NjEwLTkwOWYtYzk5ZmQyYjcxY2Nl?sa=X &ved=0CAUQkfYCahcKEwj4lr_wwtn3AhUAAAAAHQA AAAQAQ.

CHAPTER 8: EMBRACING YOUR MAIN CHARACTER ENERGY

1. Sanders, Michael, 'More Evidence on the Power of Role Models', The Behavioural Insights Team (31 July 2017). https://www.bi.team/blogs/more-evidence-on-the-power-of-role-models/.

2. Bayern, Macy, 'Women Are 21% Less Likely To Be Promoted Than Male Coworkers', TechRepublic (28 November 2018). https://www.techrepublic.com/article/women-are-21-less-likely-to-be-promoted-than-male-coworkers/.

3. Correll, Shelley J. and Mackenzie, Lori N., 'To Succeed in Tech, Women Need More Visibility', *Harvard Business Review* (13 September 2016). https://hbr.org/2016/09/to-succeed-in-tech-women-need-more-visibility.

4. Phelan, Julie E. et al., 'Competent Yet Out in the Cold: Shifting Criteria for Hiring Reflect Backlash Toward Agentic Women', *Psychology of Women Quarterly*, 32 (2008). DOI:10.1111/j.1471-6402.2008.00454.x; Rudman, Laurie A. and Peter Glick 'Prescriptive Gender Stereotypes and Backlash Toward Agentic Women', Journal of Social Issues, 57 (2002). DOI: 10.1111/0022-4537.00239.

5. 'Share of Individuals Using the Internet To Find Information About Goods and Services in the United Kingdom (UK) From 2007 to 2020', Statista (2021). https://www.statista.com/statistics/381166/researching-goods-and-services-online-in-the-uk/.

6. Salm, Lauren, '70% of Employers Are Snooping Candidates' Social Media Profiles', CareerBuilder (15 June 2017). https://www.careerbuilder.com/advice/social-media-survey-2017.

FURTHER READING

Adegoke, Yomi, and Elizabeth Uviebinené, *Slay in your lane: The Black Girl Bible* (Fourth Estate, 2018).

Bellet, Emilie, *You're Not Broke, You're Pre-Rich* (Brazen, 2021).

Beverley, Grace, *Working Hard, Hardly Working* (Hutchinson, 2021).

Brown, Brene, *Daring Greatly* (Penguin Life, 2015).

Cain, Susan, *Quiet Power* (Penguin Life, 2017).

Clear, James, *Atomic Habits* (Random House Business, 2018).

Dalton-Smith, Saundra, MD, *Sacred Rest: Recover Your Life, Renew Your Energy, Renew Your Sanity* (FaithWords, 2019).

Eggerue, Chidera, *What a Time to Be Alone* (Quadrille Publishing Ltd, 2018).

Forleo, Marie, *Everything Is Figureoutable* (Penguin, 2020).

Gannon, Emma, *The Multi-Hyphen Method* (Hodder, 2019).

Lakhiani, Vishen, *The Code of the Extraordinary Mind* (Bantam, 2019).

Maltz, Maxwell, *Psycho-Cybernetics* (Perigee Books, 2015).

Pressfield, Steven, *The War of Art: Break Through the Blocks and Win Your Inner Creative Battles* (Black Irish Entertainment, 2012).

Seal, Clare, *Real Life Money* (Headline Home, 2020).

Shetty, Jay, *Think Like a Monk* (Thorsons, 2020).

Smith, Dr Julie, *Why Has Nobody Told Me This Before?* (Michael Joseph, 2022).

Sol, Bola, *How To Save It: Fix Your Finances* (Merky Books, 2021).

Tone, Toni, *I Wish I Knew This Earlier* (Fourth Estate, 2021).

Yeboah, Stephanie, *Fattily Ever After* (Hardie Grant Books, 2020).

Young, Valerie, *The Secret Thoughts of Successful Women* (Crown Publishing Group, 2011).

INDEX